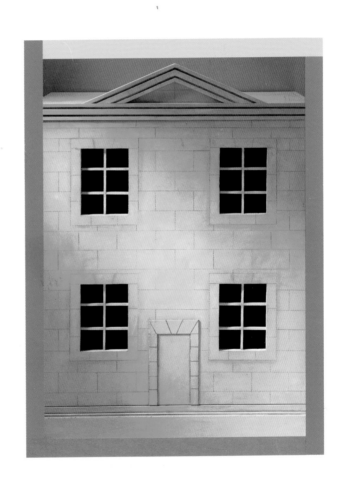

TERENCE CONRAN

CHILDREN'S FURNITURE AND TOYS

STYLISH PROJECTS
TO MAKE FOR YOUR CHILDREN

CONSULTANT EDITORS
**JOHN McGOWAN
& ROGER DuBERN**

PROJECT PHOTOGRAPHY
RICHARD FOSTER

COLLIER BOOKS
MACMILLAN PUBLISHING COMPANY / NEW YORK

MAXWELL MACMILLAN INTERNATIONAL
NEW YORK OXFORD SINGAPORE SYDNEY

For Sebastian, Jasper, Tom, Sophie, Ned, and Sam

SPECIAL NOTE

Before embarking on any of the projects in this book, you must check the law concerning building regulations and planning. It is also important that you obtain specialist advice on plumbing and electricity before attempting any alterations to these services yourself.

While every effort has been made to ensure that the information contained in this book is correct, the publisher cannot be held responsible for any loss, damage, or injury caused by reliance upon the accuracy of such information.

SAFETY

The publisher would like to thank the ROYAL SOCIETY FOR THE PREVENTION OF ACCIDENTS for reading through and checking the project instructions; their recommendations have been incorporated into the text.

Additionally, on page 125 there is a summary of the most important points relating to remodeling, safety, and the design and construction of toys and children's furniture including the latest recommendations of the U.S. Consumer Product Safety Commission. It is strongly recommended that you read this summary before making any of the projects in this book.

DIMENSIONS

Dimensions are given in U.S. measurements followed by an approximate conversion to metric. Never mix U.S. measurements and metric when making a calculation or building a project.

First published in the UK in 1992 by
Conran Octopus Limited
37 Shelton Street, London WC2H 9HN

Copyright © 1992 Conran Octopus Limited

Collier Books
Macmillan Publishing Company
866 Third Avenue
New York, NY 10022

Macmillan Publishing Company is part of the Maxwell Communication Group of Companies.

Macmillan books are available at special discounts for bulk purchases for sales promotions, premiums, fund-raising, or educational use. For details, contact:

Special Sales Director
Macmillan Publishing Company
866 Third Avenue
New York, NY 10022

First Collier Books Edition 1992
10 9 8 7 6 5 4 3 2 1

Library of Congress Cataloging-in-Publication Data

Conran, Terence.
    Children's furniture and toys : stylish projects to make for your children / Terence Conran.
      p.   cm.
    Includes index.
    ISBN 0-02-042745-X
    1. Children's furniture.   2. Wooden toy making. I. Title.
TT197.5.C5C66   1992
684′.08—dc20   92-154244
                       CIP

The designs for the projects on pages 20–5, 26–31, 32–7, 38–41, 52–7, 58–63, 64–73, 74–9, 80–9, 96–104 and 104–9 are copyright © 1992 Sir Terence Conran and may be built for personal use only.

All projects were specially built by SEAN SUTCLIFFE of Benchmark Woodworking Limited.

Typeset by Servis Filmsetting Limited, Manchester. Printed and bound in China.

Project Editor SIMON WILLIS
Consultant Editors JOHN McGOWAN
                and ROGER DuBERN
Copy Editor JACKIE MATTHEWS
Contributing Editor ELIZABETH WILHIDE
Editorial Assistant MICHAEL WILLIAMS
American Editor NATALIE CHAPMAN
Americanization EMILY VAN NESS

Art Editor HELEN LEWIS
Illustrator PAUL BRYANT
Visualizer JEAN MORLEY

Project Sketches SIR TERENCE CONRAN

Production Manager SONYA SIBBONS
Picture Researcher NADINE BAZAR

PROJECT PHOTOGRAPHY

Photography RICHARD FOSTER
Assisted by SIMON ARCHER
Art Direction CLAIRE LLOYD
Assisted by LINDY TROST
Set Building WILF DECORATION
Set Decoration MATTHEW USMAR LAUDER

CONTENTS

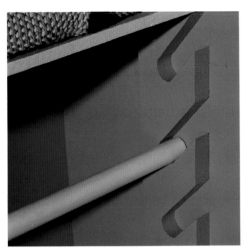 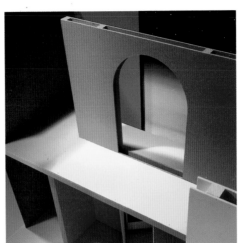 

INTRODUCTION

A child's room is a world in microcosm. There is no doubt that many of our first impressions of color, texture, design, and pattern are formed here, surrounded by the familiar everyday objects of the nursery. Most of us can vividly recall the rooms we grew up in; and we may well remember a favorite chair or a desk with as much affection as a beloved train set, doll's house, or teddy bear.

Although few people would dispute the importance of these early experiences, the design and furnishing of children's rooms and play spaces do not always bear witness to this fact. Children, of course, grow up and grow out of rooms as quickly as they grow out of clothes. A baby's nursery cannot contain an active, exploring two-year-old, and what is fun and appealing at five years old is babyish and boring at ten. For some parents this is reason enough not to devote the same degree of care and finish to a child's room as they would to other rooms in the house. And many people believe that young children are so innately destructive and chaotic that good furniture and decoration would be wasted on them.

I hope that this book will help to overturn both of these misconceptions. The changing needs of the growing child present the biggest challenge to anyone designing or equipping a child's room. But, as many of the projects in this book demonstrate, with a little imagination and ingenuity it is possible to build in enough flexibility to allow a room to change with the child.

The second common belief, that children are too careless to look after things properly, is often why so many children's rooms are bland or furnished with mismatched pieces of furniture. But I believe that children only learn to look after things if they are given items that are worth looking after.

Making the furnishings yourself enables you to respond to particular requirements and is economical.

There are also more fundamental rewards: there is no better way to demonstrate your love for your children, and they will never forget the things you have made for them. If your children wonder at your creativity, so much the better: as they grow they will be more confident about developing their own skills!

Terence Conran.

INTRODUCTION

NOOKS AND CRANNIES
Built around a small bedroom fireplace, this wall of storage provides hanging space at child height, together with intriguing niches and compartments for toys, books, games, and puzzles (left).

DRESSING-UP BOX
An old tin trunk or wooden blanket box makes the perfect home for dressing-up clothes and theatrical props (below).

PLANNING FOR CHANGE

This book is intended to apply to children from birth to around 12 years of age. Within this short space of a dozen years, children grow and change rapidly. When planning a child's room, you should allow for at least three distinct phases. From birth to the toddling stage, the room should allow for a baby's daily needs to be easily met; as the child becomes mobile and toys proliferate, storage and safety are prime considerations; later, as the child develops interests and hobbies, there must be space for self-expression. Since your family may also increase, you may have to reconcile the needs of two children at different stages of development within the same area.

Early on – perhaps even before the baby has arrived – many parents lovingly equip and decorate a nursery down to the last detail. But while this is a natural impulse, it is wise to remember that babyhood is of comparitively short duration and any equipment or furniture which is too specifically geared to a particular point in a baby's or a child's development will quickly be outgrown. There is obviously less wasted time, effort, and money if you invest in furniture that is versatile enough to be used in different ways. A chest of drawers can provide a surface for changing a baby, with linen storage below, and can later be given over to clothes storage. A chest or blanket box can provide space for bedding or diapers, then later be used as a toy box, and finally store objects such as sports equipment, tapes, or magazines.

Versatility is intrinsic to many modern storage systems. At the simplest level, shelving arrangements of the metal track and bracket variety can be spaced according to the height and reach of the child and the size and shape of what is being stored. Hanging rails can be set low down at first and later moved up. A pegged rail for hanging everything from clothes to toys, Shaker style, is perhaps the simplest and most flexible arrangement of all. Each one of these adjustable systems enables you to keep the environment in the room scaled to the child without building in too much at low level which will need to be remade as the child grows.

Elements which can be changed quickly and easily are essentially decorative – a change of paint finish, curtains, or blinds can give the room a different atmosphere to suit a new stage in the child's growth. The soft pastel shades of a baby's room, for example, might give way to brighter paintbox colors for a school-age child. Children enjoy being involved in these decisions and making a contribution to the way their room looks.

SPACE PLANNING

This architect-designed warehouse conversion offered the opportunity to create new and exciting children's spaces. Within a largely open-plan layout, a more enclosed area, linked to the ground floor with a ladder, accommodates two bedrooms with internal views down into the main living room (left). Beneath the bedrooms are play spaces equipped with chairs and tables for hobbies and schoolwork (above). While such a radical restructuring of existing space may not always be possible, it is worth bearing in mind that children appreciate and enjoy unusual spaces in which to play and live.

PART 1

BEDROOMS

 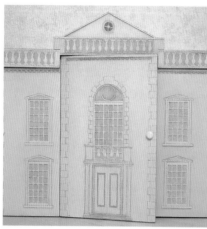 

Compared to an adult's requirements, young children make very high demands on a bedroom and spend much more of their time there. If space in the child's bedroom is restricted, toys, belongings, and noisy games quickly overrun the rest of the house. Giving the children a room which can also serve as a playroom will have a beneficial effect on the whole household. A good children's room is good for parents, too.

By the time children reach school age, they will see their bedrooms as much more than just a place to sleep in. It is a place for play, to bring friends to after school, a place in which to read and study and be surrounded by favorite things. These varied activities, together with the changes in emphasis as the child grows, call for sensitive planning and decorating.

One basic decision is which room, or rooms, of your home you allocate to the children. Children are often given the smaller bedrooms, but there is good argument, in their early years at least, for devoting a large room to the children, especially if two are sharing it; later on, when siblings need their own private space, the distribution of bedrooms can be reconsidered.

BEDROOMS

BEDS

As in any bedroom, the bed and how it is positioned is a key element in a child's room. To most children, bed is a very important place, a refuge and a source of comfort, a piece of territory which is truly their own. Although children may heartily resist being sent there at the end of the day, bed nevertheless represents a fixed point in their lives.

Whatever else changes in a child's room, it is hard to avoid two, three, or even four different types of sleeping arrangement. Although a baby isn't concerned about where it sleeps as long as it is warm and comfortable, and would probably rather be sleeping with you, it is only natural to devote a great deal of thought and care to choosing your baby's first bed. Light and portable, Moses baskets are a popular choice for the first few months and can be simply lined and trimmed in a fabric that complements the nursery decoration. A combination bassinet-carriage, also suitable for the first few months, is rather more versatile. It can be set on a stand or clipped to a wheeled frame for use as a carriage. Perhaps less practical but rather more appealing are cradles and cribs, lovingly detailed, and worth handing down from child to child. Whatever you choose, position it away from drafts and direct heat, on a stable, dust-free surface.

Your baby will outgrow its first bed fairly quickly. At this stage it is wise to invest in a strong, well-designed crib that will protect the child from accidental tumbles as its mobility increases. There is a wide variety of cribs available, made from metal or wood, with solid or railed sides, decorated or plain. Many have a "dropside" mechanism which enables the side of the crib to be lowered, making it easier to lift the baby in and out.

Research suggests that babies can see, understand, and recognize far more and at a far earlier stage than is commonly believed, which is good reason for providing them with bright and attractive shapes and colors to which they can respond. In its first year, a baby spends a significant amount of time in the crib. Suspending mobiles and other crib toys across the crib can provide some stimulation for your infant in the first months. However, for safety's sake, you are strongly advised to remove all suspended crib toys when your baby is able to push up on hands or knees or is five months of age – whichever occurs first. Bear in mind, too, that a crib full of noisy, jangling toys is not peaceful, and you may run the risk of tiring your baby rather than developing emergent senses.

A first *real* bed is a landmark and usually a source of some pride to a child. Making the transition from crib to bed often calls for an element of rearrangement and reorganization in the room and can also be the time to signal a move away from nursery furnishings. Buying an intermediate "child's bed" is often a false economy; instead choose a good-quality single bed with a firm mattress that will last for many years. Divan beds with storage drawers in the base are a practical idea and, with the addition of a tailored covering and cushions, can provide additional seating when the child is older and has friends to visit.

High sleepers – platform beds with built-in worksurfaces – appeal to a child's sense of adventure, as do bunk beds, which tend to become the focus of hours of imaginative play. Beds raised up off the floor in this fashion are potentially less safe than are conventional beds; consider installing such an arrangement only when younger siblings are well past the age when accidents are most likely to occur.

FURNISHING WITH FABRIC

Many children have to share a room at some point with a sibling. Adopting some means of dividing the room can help to ease the inevitable territorial squabbles. If you don't want to construct a permanent barrier, curtains can be an effective way of distinguishing sleeping areas from the common playing spaces (above). Fabric is a good way of dressing up a room. Cheerful red-and-yellow striped curtains are suspended from a rail by "epaulette"-style loops (right, above). A theatrical pelmet makes a grand entrance to a bedroom alcove (right, below). Twists of plain white muslin are a cheap but highly effective way of transforming a plain iron bedstead (far right).

BEDROOMS

through several stages of development. A chest of drawers, a bookcase, a set of adjustable shelves built into an alcove, a blanket box, or stacking crates can all satisfy a range of storage applications. Similarly, a hanging rail fixed at a level the child can reach, and moved up the wall as the child grows, is often more practical than a child-sized wardrobe.

DECORATION AND FURNISHING

Surfaces and finishes do need to be fairly hard-wearing in a child's room, but there is no need for them to be boring or unattractive. Practical considerations probably apply most strongly to flooring, which cannot be replaced or renovated as quickly and cheaply as wall decoration.

Pile carpeting is not a good choice, since it will inevitably become a patchwork of ugly spills and stains. Flatweave or rugged cord carpet is a better idea, while a wood floor – sanded boards or new hardwood – is warm, good-looking and practical. A large bright rag-rug or dhurrie is an economical way of adding color and pattern, but make sure it is laid over a non-slip mat to prevent falls.

For windows, blinds are neat and unobtrusive. Plain, checked, or striped curtains are also appropriate. You can match these to other soft furnishings – if there is space it's a good idea to have a chair where you can sit and read your child a bedtime story. Floor cushions, an old sofa dressed up with a bedspread, and a bedside table for an older child are also useful, if there is enough room.

Lighting should be kept simple and safe. Most small children appreciate the comforting glow of a nightlight; a new reader will welcome a bedside light. Avoid standard lamps and large table lamps which can be easily knocked over. A simple overhead fitting or a system of angled spotlights is a better option.

UP THE WALL

Wall space is put to stylish storage use in this arrangement of pegs set around the perimeter of the room, paired with a deep shelf at picture-rail height for propping up photographs and mementoes (above).

INQUIRING MIND

From an early age, most children display a deep curiosity about the world. Surround them with provocative and stimulating objects to keep their interest alive. Here a world map papers the wall, providing a background for a planet mobile and a mantelshelf array of wonderfully eclectic things to ask questions about (opposite).

STORAGE

Getting the storage arrangements right is a large part of what makes a child's room successful. In the very early days, storage should be tailored to the needs of adults using the room, making a practical and comfortable place to change, dress, and look after the baby. But, as the child grows, whatever storage you devise should allow and indeed encourage the child to participate in the process of cleaning up and taking care of possessions.

In the nursery, the greatest need is for places to store changes of bedding, diapers, and toiletries, while a drawer or simple hanging rail will usually suffice for a baby's entire wardrobe. Even so, consider buying one or two good pieces of storage furniture or setting up a flexible storage system that can see the child

BEDROOMS

PAINTED DECOR

Children's rooms lend themselves to painted decoration: it is easy, quick, and cheap to achieve, and can be brightly colored and changed with little trouble as the child grows into the next phase. Although the paint effects illustrated here are the results of many hours' work, you don't have to be a fine artist to produce lively effects – stylized patterns, "naïve" representations of animals, and simple stenciling are all quick and easy to do. A snake and a caterpillar enliven cupboard doors in a brilliantly painted room (above left), while Caribbean-style scenes dress up a plain wooden wardrobe (below center). A step beyond painted surfaces are pieces of furniture in animal shapes with painted detail, such as the enchantingly anthropomorphic work of the French artist, Gérard Rigot (above right and opposite).

CRADLE

A baby's first bed has great sentimental value. Before the baby is born, making or trimming a crib or basket is often a way for parents to express all their hopes and feelings for the future. Fathers, in particular, may take pride in fashioning their child's first bed, making their own contribution at a time when they can otherwise feel somewhat left out. And the significance of the cradle will outlast its usefulness. Later in life, the child will see the cradle as proof of the parents' concern and love and it may become an heirloom.

A rocking cradle or crib is a traditional bed for a newborn baby, the gentle lulling motion soothing and reassuring a baby unaccustomed to perfect stillness. The rockers are the most complicated part of the construction, albeit an interesting woodworking exercise. They are fashioned by gluing and clamping strips of laminated plywood together around a form to build up into curves. Holes drilled in the end panels are primarily decorative, but could also be used for suspending a soft toy or rattle.

The basic design of the cradle shown here consists of a simple pine frame, with dowels at the sides. A little care is needed to ensure that the angles are correct for insetting the plywood end panels.

The cradle is very much scaled to the first few months of a baby's life – a sense of enclosure seems to be important to a baby in its early days. But although the cradle is soon outgrown, it will find a new use when the next baby comes along. The dimensions of the cradle accommodate a standard-sized baby's mattress.

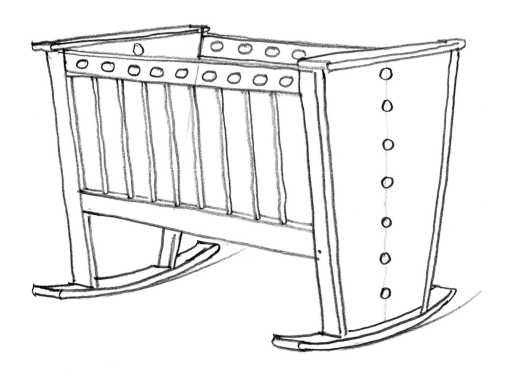

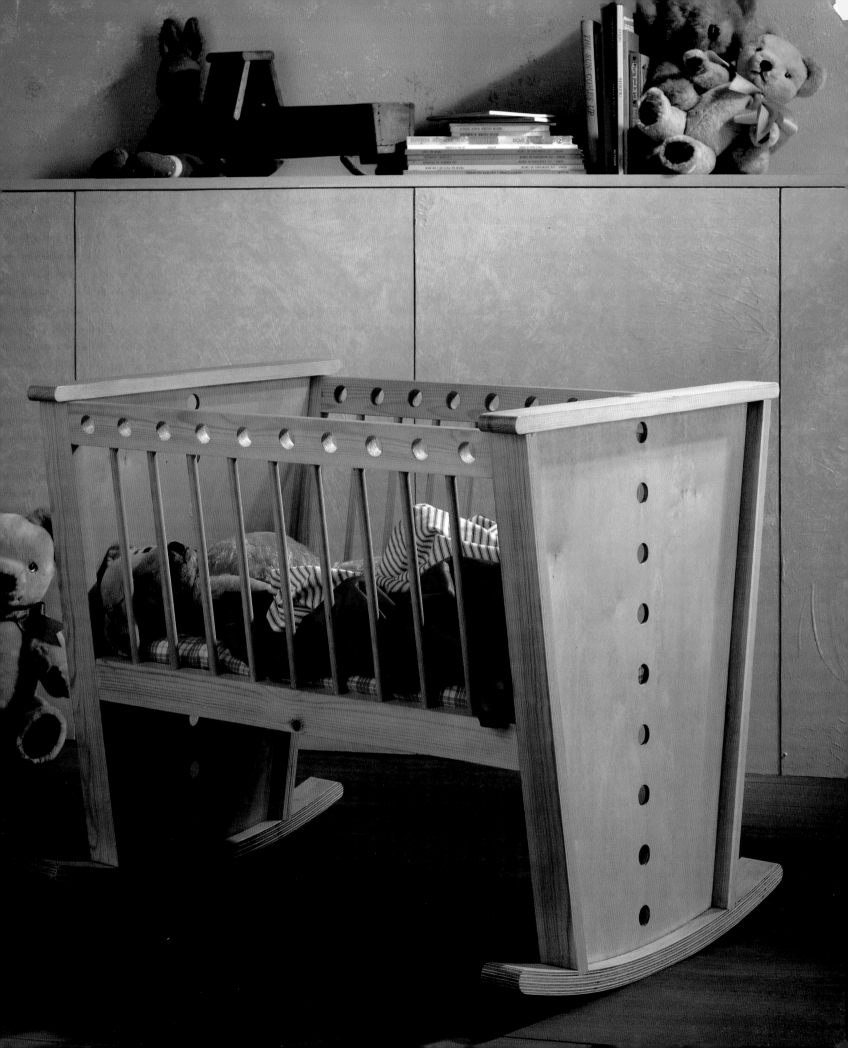

CRADLE

A new baby can easily get "lost" in a crib, and for those important first few months a bassinet or a cradle is a must. Our cradle is equipped with curved rockers that allow it to be rocked from side to side. Cradle mattresses are available from baby shops, and our design is based around a mattress measuring $13\frac{3}{4} \times 28\frac{3}{4}$in ($350 \times 730$mm).

For safety's sake, do not attempt to modify or alter the design. The size of the rockers, and the height of the mattress base from the ground,

MATERIALS

Part	Quantity	Material	Length
UPRIGHT	4	1×3in (25×75mm) S4S softwood, reduced to $2\frac{3}{16}$in (55mm) wide	$24\frac{5}{8}$in (625mm)
RAIL	4	As above	$27\frac{1}{2}$in (700mm)
CAPPING BOARD	2	As above	23in (about 580mm)
SLAT	18	$\frac{1}{2}$in (12mm) hardwood dowel	12in (300mm)
END PANEL	2	$\frac{1}{4}$in (6mm) plywood	$25\frac{1}{4}$in (640mm) high $\times\ 20\frac{3}{16}$in (512mm) wide at the top $\times\ 12\frac{1}{4}$in (312mm) wide at the bottom
ROCKER	2	Each formed from 4 pieces of $\frac{1}{4}$in (6mm) laminated plywood	Cut from a sheet approx. $2\frac{1}{4} \times 25\frac{5}{8}$in ($58 \times 650$mm)
BASE	1	$\frac{1}{4}$in (6mm) plywood	Cut to fit (approx. $15\frac{1}{4} \times 29\frac{1}{2}$in [$385 \times 750$mm])
BASE-SUPPORT BATTEN	2	1×1in (25×25mm) S4S softwood	Cut to fit (approx. $29\frac{1}{2}$in [750mm])
DOWEL (for joints)	24	$\frac{3}{8}$in (10mm) diameter	

Also required: $\frac{3}{4}$in (18mm) particleboard, to make form for rockers

have been carefully worked out to ensure stability. And the spacing between the dowels which form the sides of the cradle ensures that a baby's head, hands, and feet cannot become trapped. Similarly, the holes in the end panels and top side rails must be 1in (25mm) in diameter so that little fingers cannot become caught in them.

The main frame of the cradle is made from $1 \times 2\frac{5}{16}$in (25×55mm) S4S (smooth 4 sides) softwood. You will not be able to buy this size "off the shelf," so buy 1×3in (25×75mm) softwood and cut this stock down to size using a circular saw, or ask the supplier to do this for you. The newly sawn edge will need to be planed smooth.

The sides are formed using $\frac{1}{2}$in (12mm) hardwood dowels, and the end panels and cradle base are cut from $\frac{1}{4}$in (6mm) plywood. Choose the plywood carefully, especially if the cradle is to be given a clear finish (for this you will need a "faced" or veneered plywood). Stops could be fitted beneath the rockers to prevent any risk of tipping.

CONSTRUCTION

Cut down the softwood framing pieces and plane to finish $2\frac{3}{16}$in (55mm) wide. Then cut all the main components (that is, the uprights, rails, and slats) to length.

SIDE FRAMES

Each side of the cradle is constructed from nine slats of doweling fitted vertically between two horizontal rails (fig. 1). Along the center line of a narrow edge of one rail, mark positions for nine holes, spaced equally at $2\frac{3}{4}$in (70mm) centers. Clamp all four rails together side by side and transfer the marks from the first rail to the other three rails.

Fit a $\frac{1}{2}$in (12mm) brad-point bit in an electric drill, and drill a hole at each mark on the rails to a depth of $\frac{3}{8}$in (10mm). This is best done with the drill held upright in a drill stand. Alternatively, you can clamp the four rails firmly to a workbench.

Apply a little adhesive to each hole and assemble the two sides. Fit the dowels between two rails and

tap them together with a mallet, using scrap wood to protect the surface of the rails from the mallet blows. Lay the side frames on a flat surface for about six hours until the adhesive has firmly set.

① Making the Side Frames
Nine holes spaced at $2\frac{3}{4}$in (70mm) centers are drilled along top and bottom rails to take dowel "slats."

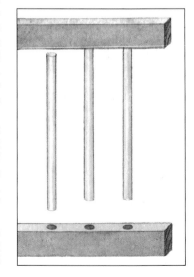

CRADLE ASSEMBLY

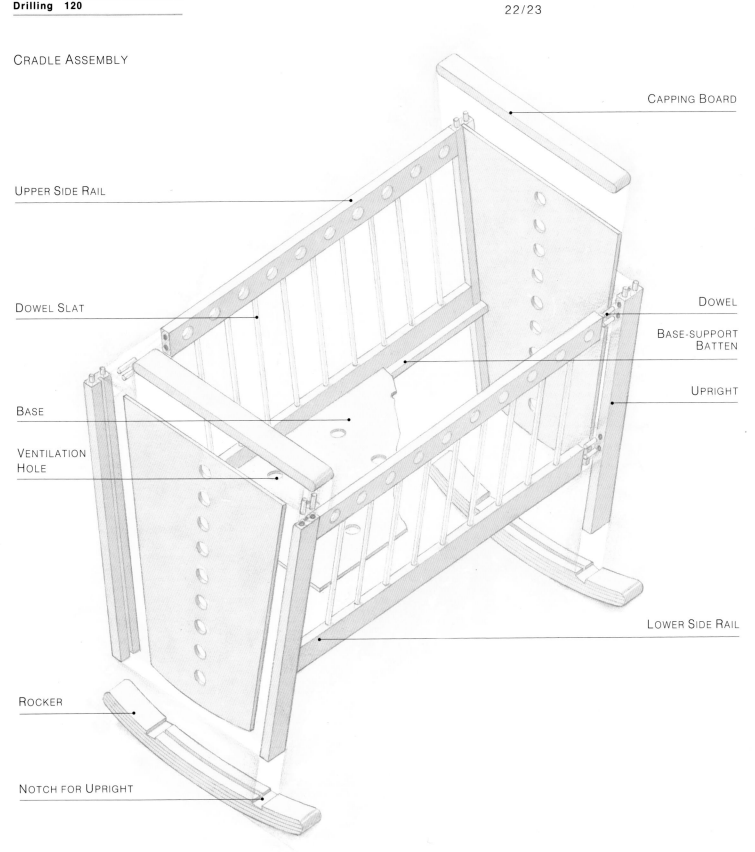

CAPPING BOARD

UPPER SIDE RAIL

DOWEL SLAT

DOWEL

BASE-SUPPORT BATTEN

UPRIGHT

BASE

VENTILATION HOLE

LOWER SIDE RAIL

ROCKER

NOTCH FOR UPRIGHT

CRADLE

UPRIGHTS

Down the length of the center of the inside face of each upright rout a $\frac{1}{4} \times \frac{1}{4}$in (6mm × 6mm) groove.

The four uprights are joined to the rails of the assembled side frames using two dowels at each joint (fig. 1). Lay the side panels flat on the bench with an upright at each end and mark the four joint positions for each panel – the tops of the uprights must be flush with the tops of the upper side rails. Using a doweling jig, drill out two holes for $\frac{3}{8}$in (10mm) dowels in the end of each rail and in matching positions in the uprights. Dry assemble to test the fit. Then apply a little adhesive to the holes of the joints, insert the dowels, and tap the uprights in place with a mallet, using a piece of scrap wood to protect the surfaces (fig. 2).

MAKING THE ROCKERS

The rockers are each made by laminating four strips of plywood bent around a particleboard form – any $\frac{3}{4}$in (18mm) offcuts will do – to make the curve (fig. 3).

The radius for the arc of the rocker form is 38in (approximately 960mm). The best way to mark this curve is to use a pencil tied to a suitable length of string attached to a nail at a central point. Mark the arc onto a piece of $\frac{3}{4}$in (18mm) particleboard measuring approximately 12 × 28in (300 × 700mm), and cut the curve using a saber saw.

Build up the thickness of the form at the curved edge using two extra pieces of board (about 6 × 28in [150 × 700mm]) to bring the thickness of the curve to $2\frac{1}{4}$in (54mm). Screw the three pieces together (fig. 3, below).

From the $\frac{1}{4}$in (6mm) plywood, cut the eight strips, each 650mm ($25\frac{5}{8}$in) long, to form the rockers. Cutting these to $2\frac{3}{8}$in (58mm) wide allows a little extra for finishing to $2\frac{3}{16}$in (55mm), which is the width of the stock used for the uprights.

Glue together the four strips to form each rocker using a non-flexible powdered resin wood glue (*not* the ready-to-use aliphatic resin type). This gives a rigid setting. Form one rocker at a time, clamping

one set around the form (fig. 3) and holding with C-clamps or a webbing clamp until the adhesive sets (about 8 hours). Then repeat for the second rocker.

END PANELS

Mark out end panels on $\frac{1}{4}$in (6mm) plywood so they are $25\frac{1}{4}$in (640mm) high, $20\frac{3}{16}$in (512mm) wide at the top and $12\frac{1}{4}$in (312mm) wide at the bottom. Check that they taper equally each side of the center line. Cut out the panels.

Line up a rocker to the bottom edge of an end panel, align the centers, and mark around the curve onto the bottom edge of the panel. Trim the panel to shape using a saber saw. Transfer the curve onto the other panel and cut this one out.

Dry assemble the end panels onto the side frames and turn the whole unit upside down.

Place one of the rockers in position alongside the end panel. Make sure the center line of the rocker lines up with the center line of the end panel. Mark on the rockers where the uprights will sit.

Using a try square, extend the marks of the upright positions across the rockers. Saw down these lines with a back saw, and chop out the notches with a chisel (*see* **Crib Assembly, page 23**).

Using a router, rout a $\frac{1}{4}$in (6mm) wide groove, $\frac{3}{8}$in (about 10mm) deep, centrally on each rocker between the notches to accept the bottom edge of the end panel.

From the underside, drill and countersink through the rockers at an angle into the uprights (fig. 4) and affix with $2\frac{1}{2}$in (64mm) No. 10 woodscrews, two to each upright. Dry assemble to check the fit.

ASSEMBLING THE BASE

Cut two base-support battens from 1 × 1in (25 × 25mm) S4S softwood, to the internal length between the end panels at the height of the lower side rail.

Plane a bevel along one length of each batten so the top edge will be horizontal to the base (fig. 5). Glue and screw the battens flush with the bottom of the lower side rail. Use $1\frac{1}{2}$in (38mm) No. 8 woodscrews.

① Joining Sides to Uprights
Mark the side rail positions on the sides of the uprights. Drill and dowel ends of rails to uprights.

② Finished Side Assembly
Note $\frac{1}{4} \times \frac{1}{4}$in (6 × 6mm) groove down center line of inside face of each upright to accept end panel.

③ Forming the Cradle Rockers
Each rocker is made from four strips of $\frac{1}{4}$in (6mm) plywood, which are bent around a purpose-cut particleboard form with a radius of 38in (960mm). The plywood strips are glued and clamped together until the adhesive sets.

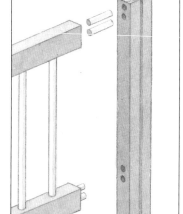

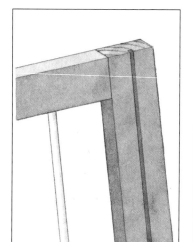

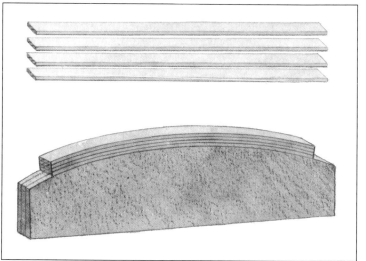

Check that the diagonals are equal to ensure the cradle is square, pulling it to adjust if necessary. Then take the internal measurements of the cradle, and cut the plywood base panel to fit. Once in place, the base will hold the cradle square.

CAPPING BOARDS

Remove the end panels and plane the top edges of the side frames so they are horizontal. Plane from the ends toward the middle to avoid splintering the outside edges of the uprights. Replace the end panels.

Cut the two capping boards to length. At the ends these will be dowel jointed to the uprights (fig. 6), but between these dowel positions a $\frac{1}{4} \times \frac{1}{4}$in (6mm × 6mm) groove, $20\frac{3}{16}$in (512mm) long, will be required centrally along the underside of each capping board to take the top edge of the end panel.

Drill down into the uprights and up into the underside of the capping boards to take the dowels and dry assemble with $\frac{3}{8}$in (10mm) dowels, two to each upright. A doweling jig may make drilling more accurate.

DECORATIVE HOLES

Take the cradle apart, and with the relevant parts held on scrap wood, drill 1in (25mm) diameter holes centrally down the end panels at $2\frac{3}{4}$in (70mm) centers.

Drill 1in (25mm) holes through the top rails, spacing these between the slats (see **Cradle Assembly, page 23**). Do not hang toys or other objects between the holes as there is a risk of strangulation.

In the base panel drill 12 ventilation holes (four rows of three holes), again to a diameter of 1in (25mm).

FINAL ASSEMBLY

With a sanding block or finishing sander, round off the ends of the rockers and capping boards.

Glue up the cradle in the following order: (1) end panels to side frames; (2) rockers to base of end panels; (3) capping boards to top of end panels. Finally, simply drop the base panel into place.

Before applying your finish, make sure all edges and holes are rounded and sanded smooth.

4 Fitting the Rockers to the Uprights and End Panels
Locate the end panels in the uprights and turn the cradle upside down. Cut notches in the rockers to accept the ends of the uprights and rout grooves to accept the end panels. Screw through underside of rockers into each upright.

5 Base-support Battens
Cut battens to internal lengths between end panels. Screw in place, flush with lower side rail.

6 Fitting the Capping Board
Rout underside of capping board to accept top of end panel. Dowel capping board ends to uprights.

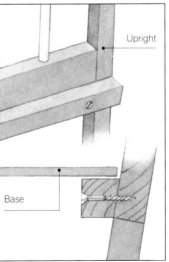

Upright

Base

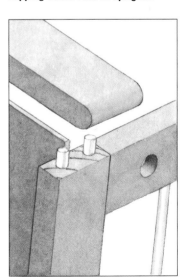

ROCKING CHAIR

A rocking chair is a classic item of nursery furniture. An adult-sized rocker is an ideal place for reading a bedtime story to a sleepy child. But a small, specially made rocking chair, such as the one shown here, has much more personal meaning and appeal for the child itself. Having a chair of one's own is something to be proud of, a symbol of childhood that is accorded special significance and often cherished for many years to come.

The design and construction of this rocking chair are fairly straightforward. The most complicated part of making it consists of shaping the rockers which are built up from strips of plywood. The rest of the chair is also made of plywood, saber sawed into the appropriate shapes. The plywood provides an easy surface to decorate. The chair could be painted a color to complement the room, and you might add a cushion for extra comfort.

Wit and humor are important elements that should not be overlooked in designs for children's furniture. The rounded wings of the rocker, which resemble great Mickey Mouse ears, are vaguely anthropomorphic, a quality accentuated further by the two "eye-holes" drilled through the back. Chairs which wrap around and encircle a child in this way make a cozy place to sit and offer a pleasing sense of security.

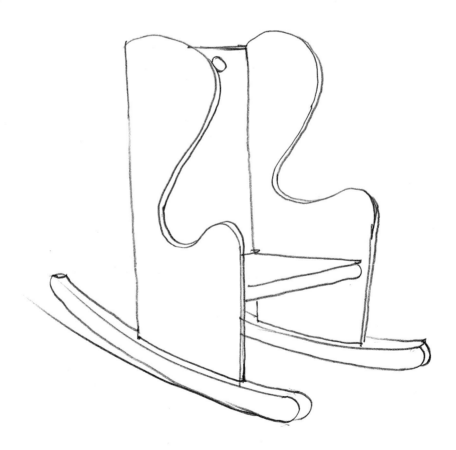

ROCKING CHAIR

Even small children eventually stop running around to take a breather, and when they do it is a good idea for them to have their own comfortable chair where they can rest and relax, read, or watch television. The child's rocking chair made here is ideal. The chair is about $27\frac{1}{2}$in (700mm) high overall, and it is perfect for children aged about four years old. The entire chair is made from $\frac{3}{8}$in (9mm) plywood. You only need a sheet measuring 3×5ft (about 910×1400mm), but you may end up having to buy a sheet of ply that measures 3×6ft (910×1800mm), which is more commonly available. However, many stockists will saw plywood to the size that you require.

TOOLS

WORKBENCH (fixed or portable)

UTILITY KNIFE

STEEL MEASURING TAPE

STEEL RULE

TRY SQUARE

MARKING GAUGE

PANEL SAW or CIRCULAR POWER SAW

POWER DRILL

SPADE BIT – 1in (25mm), to cut holes in back panel

2 C-CLAMPS

2 SASH CLAMPS or WEBBING CLAMP

SMOOTHING PLANE

POWER ROUTER and $\frac{1}{4}$in (6mm) STRAIGHT BIT

ROUNDING-OVER CUTTER for router (or plane, surform tool, or sanding block)

POWER FINISHING SANDER or HAND SANDING BLOCK

SABER SAW or SURFORM TOOL

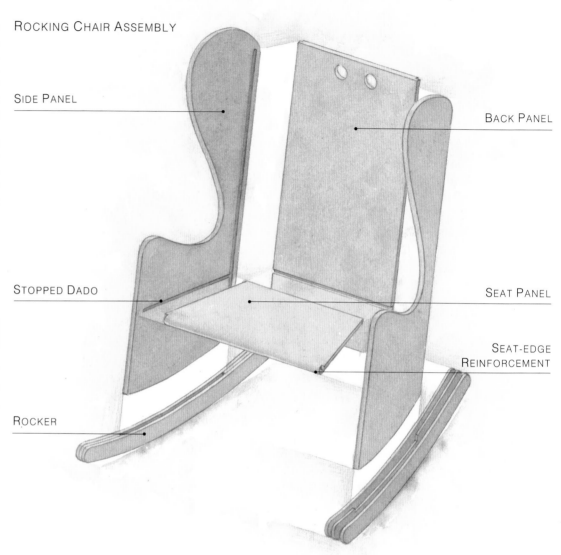

ROCKING CHAIR ASSEMBLY

SIDE PANEL

BACK PANEL

STOPPED DADO

SEAT PANEL

SEAT-EDGE REINFORCEMENT

ROCKER

MATERIALS

Part	Quantity	Material	Length
SIDE PANEL	2	$\frac{3}{8}$in (9mm) plywood	Cut from a sheet $13 \times 27\frac{1}{2}$in (320×700mm)*
BACK PANEL	1	As above	$10\frac{1}{4} \times 23\frac{5}{8}$in ($260 \times 600$mm)
SEAT PANEL	1	As above	$11\frac{5}{8}$in (296mm) deep $\times 12\frac{1}{4}$in (310mm) wide (tapering to $10\frac{1}{4}$in [260mm] at the back)
SEAT-EDGE REINFORCEMENT	1	As above	$2 \times 12\frac{1}{4}$in (50×310mm)
ROCKER	2	Each formed from 3 pieces of $\frac{3}{8}$in (9mm) plywood	Cut from a sheet approx. $15\frac{3}{4} \times 26$in (400×660mm)*

* Cut from grid pattern provided on page 29

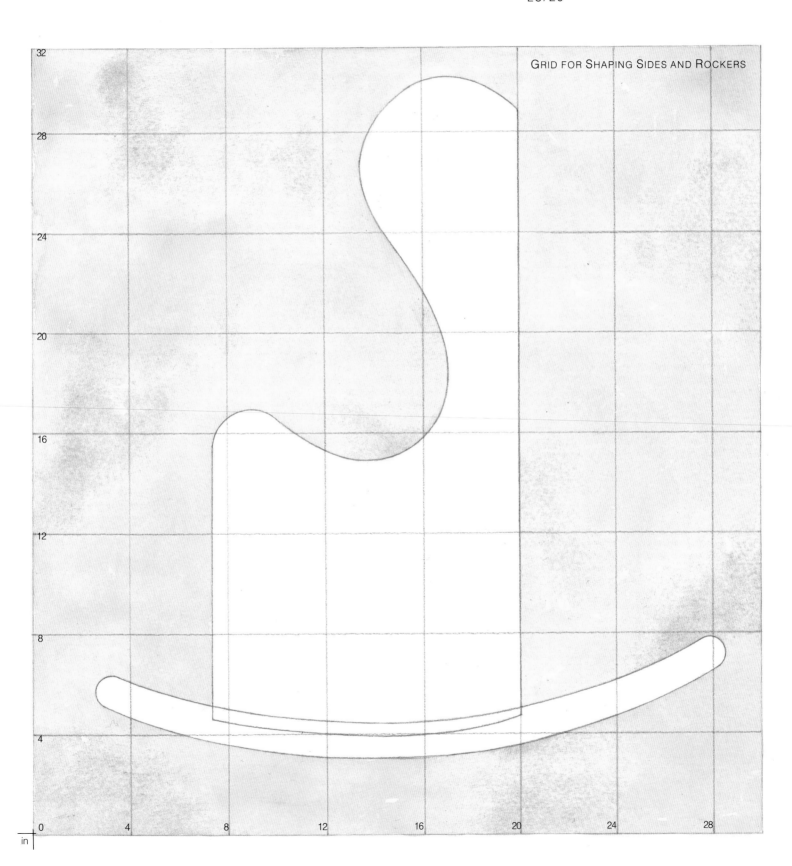

GRID FOR SHAPING SIDES AND ROCKERS

ROCKING CHAIR

CONSTRUCTION

Mark out the main pieces for the sides, back, and seat on the $\frac{3}{8}$in (9mm) plywood sheet. Double check the measurements are accurate, then cut out the pieces using a saber saw or a circular saw.

SHAPING THE SEAT

Mark out the front of the seat so that it measures $12\frac{1}{4}$in (310mm) wide at the front, narrowing evenly at each side to $10\frac{1}{4}$in (260mm) wide at the back. The front-to-back measurement is $11\frac{5}{8}$in (296mm). When you are sure that the seat is a regular shape, cut it out using a saber saw or a circular power saw.

SHAPING THE SIDES

Using the grid (page 29), transfer the shape of the side panel and rocker onto a large sheet of paper. Brown paper is ideal for the pattern, but newspaper will do.

Once you are satisfied with the shape of the side (it doesn't have to be *exactly* as shown here), transfer the outline to one of the plywood side panels. The easiest way to do this is first to trace over the drawn outline on the *reverse* side of the paper using a soft pencil, then lay the paper pattern onto the plywood panel the right way up and secure it down at the sides and corners with adhesive tape. Now go over the outline again, pressing hard with the pencil. The outline will be transferred onto the wood.

Cut out the shape using a saber saw, and sand the edges smooth. Lay this shaped piece on top of the plywood for the second side panel, draw around it, and cut out and smooth as before.

SHAPING THE ROCKERS

Each rocker is made from three thicknesses of plywood, so you have to cut out six shapes in total. Following the method described above for the side panel, transfer the pattern of the rocker onto the plywood sheet set aside for the rockers and cut out the first rocker piece using a saber saw. Sand or plane this accurately to shape as shown on the grid

(page 29). The concave (upper) edge can be shaped using either a saber saw or a surform tool.

Use this first rocker section as a template to mark out the other five pieces on the plywood panel. Cut all of these out with a saber saw and sand all the edges smooth.

MAKING THE ROCKERS

The rockers are made by laminating three shaped pieces of plywood together. Before this is done, the two central pieces are notched to create slots to take the side panels (fig. 1). To mark out on the central pieces, hold one of the shaped pieces against a side panel, referring to the grid to position it correctly. The rocker should protrude about $4\frac{3}{4}$in (120mm) in front of the panel and $8\frac{5}{8}$in (220mm) behind it.

Mark off the width of the side panel onto the concave edge of a rocker strip. Cut out a $\frac{1}{2}$in (12mm) deep section across the full thickness between these marks, following the curve of the bottom edge of the side panel. Repeat the process on another rocker strip.

Glue up each set of three strips, with one whole rocker on each side of the slotted rocker (fig. 1, below). Clamp together and, when the adhesive has set, round off the ends and sand the surfaces flush. Stops could be added to prevent tipping.

MAKING THE DADOS FOR THE BACK PANEL

The back and seat panels fit into dados (slots) which must be cut in the inside faces of the side panels. A typical section of this, with dimensions marked, is shown (fig. 2). Both the back panel and the seat panel are rabbeted along their sides to fit snugly into the dados.

To mark out the back dado on the side panel, measure and draw a line $\frac{5}{8}$in (15mm) in from the back edge of the panel (fig. 3). This marks the front edge of the dado. Mark a parallel line $\frac{1}{4}$in (6mm) toward the back edge using a marking gauge; this line marks the dado width for the back panel.

To determine the length of the dado, place a side panel into a rocker and offer up the back panel

---

1 Forming the Rockers
Each rocker is made from three pieces of plywood; notch central piece to accept chair side panel.

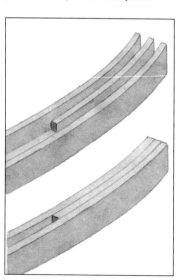

2 Dado and Rabbet Detail
The main chair parts are joined using $\frac{3}{16} \times \frac{1}{4}$in (5 × 6mm) dados and matching rabbets as shown.

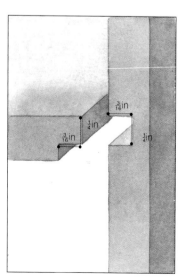

3 Back and Side Panels
Rout dado to accept back panel rabbet $\frac{5}{8}$in (15mm) from and parallel with back of side panel.

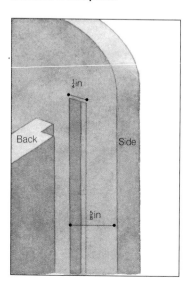

4 Seat and Back Panels
Rout a dado 6in (150mm) up from bottom of back panel to accept rabbet in back edge of seat panel.

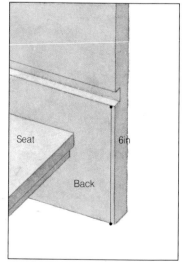

so that it comes just above the rocker. Mark off the top and bottom of the back panel across the marked lines to indicate the length of the dado.

Make corresponding marks for the dado on the other side panel. (Remember they must be mirror images of each other.)

CUTTING THE DADOS FOR THE SEAT

Measure 6in (150mm) up from the bottom edge of the back panel and, using a marking gauge, mark off a $\frac{1}{4}$in (6mm) wide dado for where the seat panel will be rabbeted to join the back panel (fig. 4).

Offer up the back panel to each of the side panels and transfer marks for the height of the seat panel on to the side panels. Offer up the seat panel to each side panel at this height, positioned at 90 degrees to the dado marks for the back panel (fig. 5), and measure for the length of the seat dado on the side panel so that, when it is cut, a $\frac{1}{4}$in (6mm) stopped shoulder will be left at the front of the seat (fig. 6).

Mark the dado for the seat on the inside face of the other side panel in the same way.

Cut out all the dados using a router fitted with a $\frac{1}{4}$in (6mm) wide straight-cutting bit set to cut to a depth of $\frac{3}{16}$in (5mm).

CUTTING THE RABBETS IN THE SEAT AND BACK PANELS

To fit into the dados, the tongues in the seat and back panels must be $\frac{1}{4}$in (6mm) wide and $\frac{3}{16}$in (5mm) deep. To ensure the panels are a tight fit you will need to rout rabbets $\frac{3}{16}$in (5mm) wide and to a depth so that they leave $\frac{1}{4}$in (6mm) of fixed tongue to fit into the housing. Practice the routing technique first on plywood scraps to get the fit right, then rout around the back and sides of the seat panel underside, remembering to leave the $\frac{1}{4}$in (6mm) stopped shoulder at the front of the seat (fig. 6). Also rout a rabbet down the reverse side of the long edges of the back panel (that is, the side that does not have any seat dado cut into it) (fig. 3).

FINISHING

Drill two 1in (25mm) diameter holes through the back panel, about 1$\frac{3}{8}$in (35mm) down from the top edge to the centers of the holes and about 1$\frac{3}{8}$in (35mm) apart, center to center. These holes are decorative and are useful for lifting the chair.

Rub down all the panels with sandpaper until smooth. Dry assemble them to check the fit.

For aesthetic reasons, glue and nail a strip of 2in (50mm) wide plywood offcut to the underside of the front of the seat panel (fig. 7).

Using a rounding-over cutter fitted in a router, or surform tool, or sanding block, round off the front edge of the seat, the edges of the seat-reinforcing strip, the top and bottom edges of the back panel, all around the shaped side panels, and the inside of the holes, so that all exposed edges are smooth.

Apply adhesive to the dados and assemble all the components, holding the seat together with sash clamps or a webbing clamp.

Finish the chair as required.

5 Seat and Side Panels
Mark back panel dado position on side panels. Rout dados for seat at right angles to marked points.

6 Seat Panel Rabbets
Rout $\frac{3}{16} \times \frac{1}{4}$in (5 × 6mm) rabbets along back and side edges. Rabbets at sides are stopped $\frac{1}{4}$in (6mm) short.

7 Seat-edge Reinforcement
Glue and nail an offcut to underside of seat panel, flush with front edge. Round over front edge to finish off.

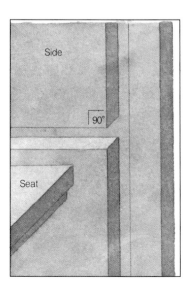

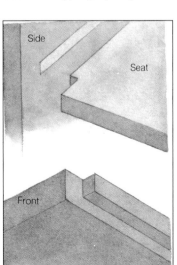

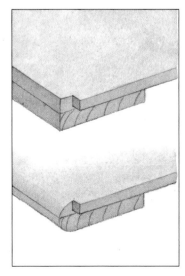

STORAGE HOUSE

Play and practicality come together in this witty "doll's house" storage structure, designed to encourage children to participate in tidying up and taking care of their own things, while helping to make a game of it. Attractive, interesting, and amusing storage like this not only enlivens a bedroom but is fun to use, and this house, with its opening windows and doors, helps to teach children to put back their toys and other belongings literally "where they live."

The construction demands only the most basic woodworking skills. There are only a few angles or curves, and the main framework consists of straight panels made of MDF (medium-density fiberboard). The house here is built into a recess but it could equally be free-standing or set against a wall without being retained on either side. Down the center of the house, the arches over the windows are cut out to make handles to open either hinged doors or box drawers.

The house can be decorated entirely to your own architectural preferences. If you aren't confident about your painting skills, you can make a window stencil and a door stencil and use these as templates to ensure uniformity of design, or you could cut out squares of paper and glue these on top to make window panes or door shapes, varnishing over the top so they don't peel away. Inside, storage spaces can be left plain or painted or papered to take the doll's house illusion a stage further.

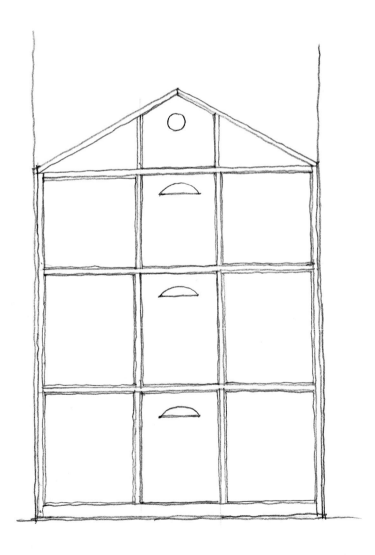

Storage House

Here is a free-standing storage unit with a difference – it is built in the shape of a town house. The storage is divided into compartments which have either conventional side-hinged doors, bottom-hinged flap-down doors, toy boxes to slide in and out, or they can be left as open shelves. For safety's sake, you should only fit toy boxes along the bottom row because these can be heavy when full.

The dimensions given are easily modified if you want a larger or smaller unit, or if it is to fit into an alcove. If it is free-standing, the storage house must be screwed to the wall through the back panel to ensure it is absolutely secure.

The cupboard is made from four 4 × 8ft (1220 × 2440mm) sheets of $\frac{5}{8}$in (15mm) MDF (medium density fiberboard); alternatively, $\frac{5}{8}$in (15mm) lumber core can be used.

Tools

WORKBENCH (fixed or portable)

STEEL MEASURING TAPE

STEEL RULE

TRY SQUARE or COMBINATION SQUARE

ADJUSTABLE BEVEL

SABER SAW or CIRCULAR POWER SAW – for cutting out panels

POWER DRILL

DRILL BIT – $\frac{1}{8}$in (3mm)

COUNTERSINK BIT

HOLE SAW – 2in (50mm) diameter

SCREWDRIVER

CLAW HAMMER

SMOOTHING PLANE

ROUTER

STRAIGHT BIT – $\frac{5}{8}$in (15mm)

C-CLAMPS

POWER SANDER or HAND SANDING BLOCK

Materials

Part	Quantity	Material	Length
SIDE PANEL	2	$\frac{5}{8}$in (15mm) MDF	15 × 57$\frac{1}{2}$in (380 × 1460mm)
TOP PANEL	1	As above	15 × 47$\frac{1}{4}$in (380 × 1200mm)
BOTTOM PANEL	1	As above	As above
CENTRAL DIVIDER	2	As above	14$\frac{3}{8}$ × 56$\frac{5}{8}$in (365 × 1438mm)
OUTER SHELF	4	As above	14$\frac{3}{8}$ × 16$\frac{3}{4}$in (365 × 428mm)
INNER SHELF	2	As above	12$\frac{7}{8}$ × 14$\frac{3}{8}$in (326 × 365mm)
BACK PANEL	1	As above	47$\frac{1}{4}$ × 56$\frac{3}{4}$in (1200 × 1440mm)
ROOF PANEL	2	As above	15 × 30$\frac{3}{4}$in (380 × 780mm)
ROOF DIVIDER	2	As above	Cut from 12$\frac{1}{4}$ × 14$\frac{3}{8}$in (310 × 365mm)
ROOF BACK PANEL	1	As above	Cut from 11$\frac{7}{8}$ × 47$\frac{1}{4}$in (300 × 1200mm)
ROOF FIXING BLOCK	1	Softwood offcut	2 × 15in (50 × 380mm)
PLINTH FRONT	1	$\frac{5}{8}$in (15mm) MDF	1$\frac{9}{16}$ × 48in (40 × 1220mm)
PLINTH BACK	1	As above	As above
PLINTH SIDE	2	As above	1$\frac{9}{16}$ × 13$\frac{3}{4}$in (40 × 350mm)
OUTER DOOR	As required	As above	16$\frac{1}{2}$ × 18$\frac{1}{2}$in (420 × 470mm)*
INNER DOOR	As required	As above	12$\frac{5}{8}$ × 18$\frac{1}{2}$in (320 × 470mm)*
TOY BOX FRONT	1 per box	As above	12$\frac{5}{8}$ × 18$\frac{1}{2}$in (320 × 470mm)*
TOY BOX BACK	1 per box	As above	As above
TOY BOX SIDE	2 per box	As above	13$\frac{5}{8}$ × 18$\frac{1}{2}$in (345 × 470mm)*
TOY BOX BASE	1 per box	As above	12$\frac{1}{4}$ × 13$\frac{1}{4}$in (310 × 335mm)*

* Door and toy box sizes are approximate; pieces should be cut to fit as required to give a $\frac{1}{16}$in (1.5mm) clearance all around; the topmost inner door will need to be shaped to follow apex of roof

Carcass

Mark and cut out all of the components for the carcass – that is, the top, bottom, two sides, and two central dividers.

Side Panels

Mark and cut a $\frac{5}{8}$in (15mm) deep rabbet into the top and bottom edges of each side panel (fig. 1, page 36), using a router fitted with a $\frac{5}{8}$in (15mm) straight cutter bit.

Divide each side panel into three equal sections, then mark $\frac{5}{8}$in (15mm) wide dados centrally at these heights, across the inside face of each panel. Rout the dados to a depth of $\frac{1}{4}$in (5mm).

Top and Bottom Panels

Mark off positions for the $\frac{5}{8}$in (15mm) wide dados on the inside faces of the top and bottom panels so that there is a central section with an internal dimension of 12$\frac{5}{8}$in (320mm) wide. This leaves an internal dimension of 16$\frac{1}{2}$in (420mm) for the two outer sections.

Cut the two dados $\frac{5}{8}$in (15mm) wide and $\frac{1}{4}$in (5mm) deep across the inside face of the bottom panel (fig. 2, page 36). The top panel will be housed on both sides, so mark around for the upper dado, but this time cut the dados to a depth of $\frac{1}{8}$in (3mm) only, so the panel will not be too thin at the point where the dados have been cut.

Central Dividers

These are $\frac{7}{8}$in (22mm) shorter than the side panels. Offer one of the central dividers up to the side panel so the side panel overlaps by $\frac{3}{8}$in (10mm) at the bottom and by $\frac{1}{2}$in (12mm) at the top, and mark off the dados for the shelves (fig. 3, page 36). Square around to the sides. Mark off on to the other central divider. Cut the dados on the central dividers $\frac{5}{8}$in (15mm) wide and $\frac{1}{8}$in (3mm) deep.

Back Panel Rabbeting

Cut a rabbet $\frac{5}{8}$in (15mm) wide and $\frac{1}{4}$in (5mm) deep around the back inside faces of both side panels and the top and bottom panels.

Marking square	118
Dado joint	**123**
Rabbets	**123**

BEDROOMS
Storage House
34/35

STORAGE HOUSE ASSEMBLY

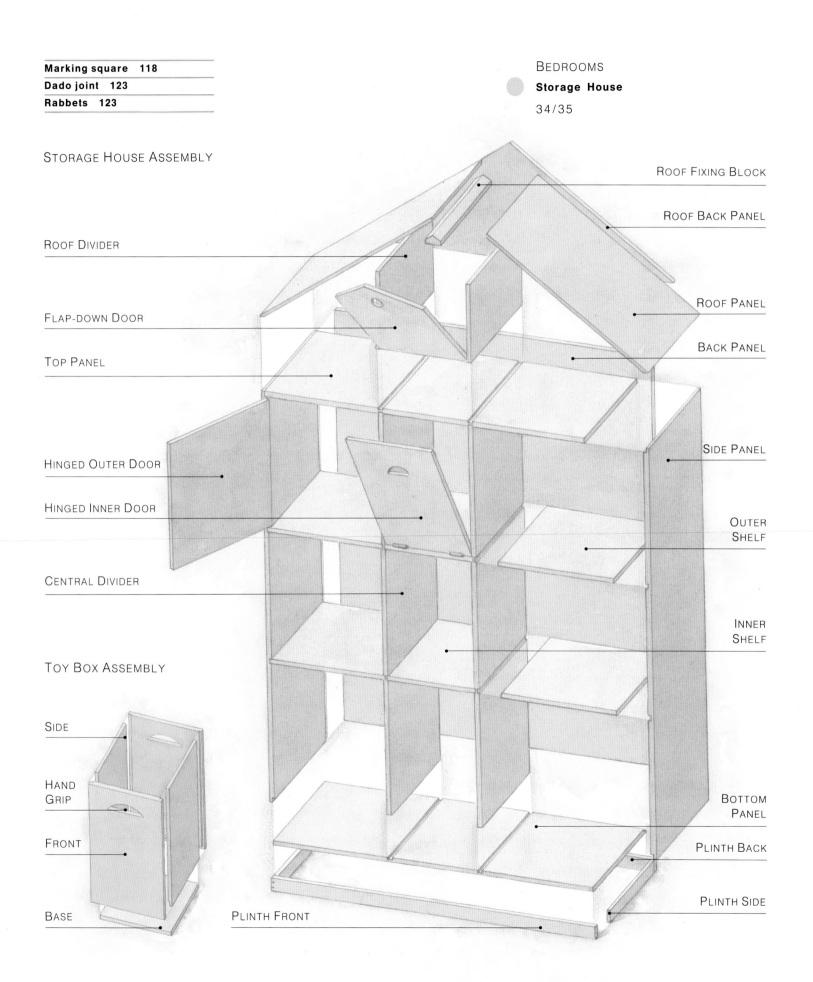

ROOF FIXING BLOCK

ROOF BACK PANEL

ROOF DIVIDER

ROOF PANEL

FLAP-DOWN DOOR

BACK PANEL

TOP PANEL

HINGED OUTER DOOR

SIDE PANEL

HINGED INNER DOOR

OUTER SHELF

CENTRAL DIVIDER

INNER SHELF

TOY BOX ASSEMBLY

SIDE

HAND GRIP

FRONT

BOTTOM PANEL

PLINTH BACK

PLINTH SIDE

BASE

PLINTH FRONT

Storage House

Assembly

Drill and countersink $\frac{1}{8}$in (3mm) holes in three places through the center line of all the rabbets on the top, bottom, and side panels. Make sure the central dividers are flush at the front. Glue and screw the carcass together – top, bottom, sides, and central dividers – using $1\frac{1}{4}$in (32mm) No. 8 woodscrews.

Check that the diagonals are equal to ensure that the carcass is absolutely square. Nail temporary battens diagonally across the front and back, to hold the carcass square while the adhesive dries.

Back Panel

Check the dimensions of the back panel from the assembled carcass, then cut out the back panel ensuring it is square.

Offer the back panel in place and mark off the positions of the central dividers from the inside to give the fixing line. Drill through the back panel from the inside, down the center of these lines in about six places spaced equally. Countersink the holes from the outside.

Drill and countersink from the outside of the back panel into the top, bottom, and sides along the center line of the back panel rabbet width in six places to fit the back panel to the carcass.

Glue and screw the back panel in place through the top, bottom, and side panels into the back, and through the back panel into the central dividers.

Shelves

Check the internal dimensions of the assembled main section and cut out the inner and outer shelves. Check the fit, then apply adhesive to the rabbets, and slide the shelves into position to line up flush with the front. Drill, countersink, and screw through the side panels into the outer shelves (fig. 4).

Plinth

Cut out the plinth components and glue and screw the side pieces between the front and back pieces with the corners flush (*see* **Storage House Assembly, page 35**).

Lay the assembled main section on its back and fit the plinth using glue blocks (offcuts) glued and screwed at intervals all around.

Roof

Roof Panels

Cut out the two roof panels to the correct width, but leave them slightly overlong for the time being. Set an adjustable bevel to 63 degrees and bevel the apex ends of the panels to this angle, either with a circular saw or a saber saw set to this angle, or plane it by hand (fig. 5).

At the eaves level, set the bevel to 27 degrees and mark off and cut the angles of the two panels.

Temporarily nail the eaves edges down into the top panel and check that the apex comes together neatly.

① **Rabbeting the Side Panels**
Cut $\frac{1}{4} \times \frac{5}{8}$in (5 × 15mm) rabbets across the top and bottom inside edges of the side panels.

Roof Dividers

Take the roof dividers and offer them up to the rabbets in the top panel, holding them at right angles to the top panel. Mark off the required length and the angle at which to cut each roof divider at the top using an adjustable bevel (fig. 6). Cut both dividers to length and carefully angle the top edges.

Remove the roof panels and drill and countersink at the eaves in three places at an angle (fig. 5). Next, drill and countersink vertically through the roof into the roof dividers in three places, making sure the dividers are flush at the front (fig. 6). Dry assemble the roof structure to the main section.

Fixing Block

Cut the roof fixing block to length, offer it up to the apex of the roof, and mark and plane off the angles of the top surfaces so the block fits neatly against the underside of the apex. Dry assemble, screwing the block up so that it is square to the roof panels (fig. 5, below).

② **Top and Bottom Dados**
Above: Rout $\frac{1}{8}$in (3mm) dados in both faces of top panel. *Below:* Rout $\frac{1}{4}$in (5mm) dados for bottom panel.

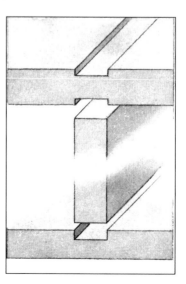

Roof Back Panel

Take the roof back panel and offer it up to the roof section, lining up the bottom edge with the top of the main back panel. Mark off the roof angles from the inside. Remove the roof back panel and cut to the marked lines so that it fits inside the roof with the back flush (*see* **Storage House Assembly, page 35**).

With the roof back panel in position, mark off the positions of the roof dividers from the inside to give a fixing line. Remove the panel, drill through from the inside in two places on each of the center lines of the dividers' positions. Countersink these holes from the back. Dry assemble the dividers.

Drill and countersink down square to the roof through the center line of the back panel thickness in four places in the top of each roof panel.

Dismantle the roof structure, glue up all the joints, and reassemble, gluing, screwing, and countersinking the back panel in place. Leave the roof structure to dry.

③ **Cutting the Central Dividers**
Hold central divider $\frac{1}{2}$in (12mm) short of top of side panel; transfer shelf dado positions to divider.

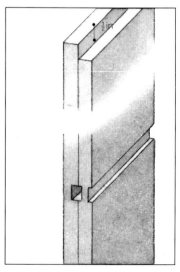

DOORS

SIDE DOORS

Measure the aperture and reduce the size by $\frac{1}{8}$in (3mm) each way to give a $\frac{1}{16}$in (1.5mm) gap all around. Cut out a door, wedge it in place so that it is perfectly square in the opening, and hang it with two flush hinges so it is flush with the front. Fix a magnetic touch-latch so the door will not need a handle.

Make and fit as many side-hinged doors as required.

FLAP-DOWN DOORS

Cut out and install the flap-down doors in the same way as the side-hinged doors, but fit the hinges on the bottom edge. Make cut-outs as handholds using a saber saw.

SHAPED FLAP-DOWN

This is shaped to fit the apex of the roof. Fit flush hinges along the bottom edge and a magnetic touch-latch to the underside of the roof fixing block. For a handhold, cut a 2in (50mm) diameter circle.

TOY BOX

The toy box simply slides in and out of the central lower or outer lower compartments. Measure the aperture, and reduce the size by $\frac{1}{8}$in (3mm) each way. Cut out the front and back panels to these dimensions. Cut $\frac{1}{4}\times\frac{5}{8}$in (5 × 15mm) rabbets down the long inside edges of the front and back panels (see **Toy Box Assembly, page 35**). Cut out the sides to the internal depth of the compartments, less $\frac{3}{8}$in (20mm).

Cut $\frac{1}{4}\times\frac{5}{8}$in (5 × 15mm) rabbets along the bottom inner edges of the front, back, and side panels. Drill and countersink through the front and back panels in four places on the center line of the side panel thickness. Glue and screw the box pieces together.

Cut the base to fit in the rabbets of the bottom of the box. Drill and countersink in three places through the side, front, and back panels to the center line of the base thickness. Glue and screw together.

Cut out the handholds in the front and back panels using a saber saw.

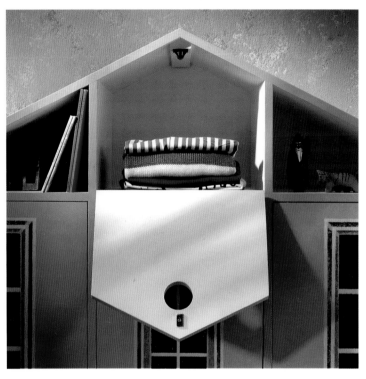

FLAP-DOWN DOORS

The flap-down door at the apex of the storage house is shaped to fit the apex of the roof. A circular cut-out provides a finger-grip opening; the magnetic catch "invisibly" holds the door shut when it's closed.

---

4 **Fitting the Shelves**
Above: Glue shelves into dados in central dividers. *Below:* Screw shelves into side panel dados.

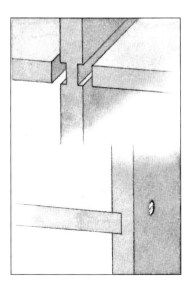

5 **Adding the Roof**
Left above: Angle apex end of roof panel at 63 degrees and other end at 27 degrees. *Right:* Nail roof in place to check the fit. *Left below:* Angle roof fixing block to fit flush with apex; screw up through block into roof panels.

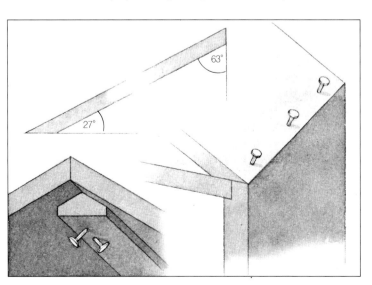

6 **Roof Dividers**
Angle top edges of roof dividers to sit flush with roof panel and screw in place, flush with front of house.

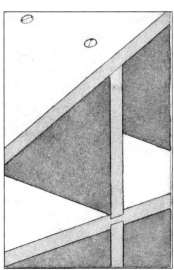

SHELF, RAIL, AND PEG STORAGE

Where it may not make sense to children to put things away, they can usually see the point of hanging things up. Children like to see their possessions about them and a wall of pegs or shelves serves as both display and storage for all those belongings that would otherwise litter the floor.

The basic design owes something to Shaker pegboards, horizontal rails for hanging things off the floor, usually applied around the perimeter of the room at picture-rail height. In this case, however, the pegs are arranged vertically; a series could be lined up to make a wall of storage, one of the simplest and most economical ways of bringing order out of chaos. And the simple rhythmic arrangement of verticals and crossbars is attractive enough in its own right, even without anything thrown over it.

Made of doweling and lengths of pine, the pegboards are very easy to make. The shelves are a variation on the same basic construction; alternatively, pegs and shelves could be combined along the same length. The pegs are angled so that they are longer at the top, shorter at the bottom, allowing each successive layer to hang free of the next.

The pegs can be mounted fairly high up the wall if you are worried that the children may try to climb up them. In any event, it is important to ensure that the screws at the top and bottom are located securely into wall anchors so that the boards are anchored to the wall.

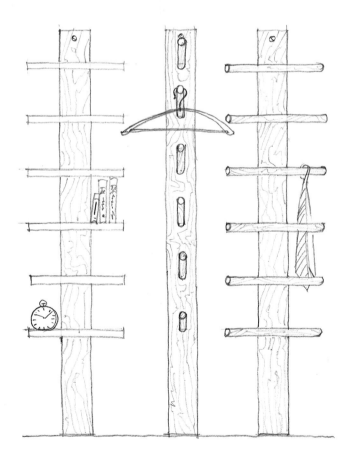

Shelf, Rail, and Peg Storage

Children tend to leave belongings, especially clothes, shoes, and toys, scattered about the floors of their rooms; but a simple and easy-to-use storage system might encourage them to be a bit more tidy. These shelves, rails, and pegs fit the bill: all are based on the same principle, and consist of a simple backboard with seven shelves, rails, or pegs down its length.

There is a risk that children will climb on these pieces. You must, therefore, screw and anchor the backboards securely to the wall, and ensure that they are placed high enough up to deter children from climbing on them, or running into the projecting pegs.

Materials

Part	Quantity	Material	Length
Shelves			
BACKBOARD	1	$1\frac{1}{4} \times 5\frac{1}{2}$in (32×140mm) S4S softwood	59in (1500mm)
SHELF	7	As above	$17\frac{3}{4}$in (450mm)
Rails			
BACKBOARD	1	$1\frac{1}{4} \times 4\frac{1}{2}$in (32×115mm) S4S softwood	59in (1500mm)
RAIL	7	1in (25mm) hardwood dowel	$17\frac{3}{4}$in (450mm)
Pegs			
BACKBOARD	1	$1\frac{1}{4} \times 4\frac{1}{2}$in (32×115mm) S4S softwood	59in (1500mm)
PEG	7	1in (25mm) hardwood dowel	From 53in (1350mm)

Tools

WORKBENCH (fixed or portable)

MAT KNIFE

STEEL MEASURING TAPE

STEEL RULE

TRY SQUARE

PANEL SAW or CIRCULAR POWER SAW

POWER DRILL

DRILL BIT – $\frac{1}{8}$in (3mm)

COUNTERSINK BIT

SCREWDRIVER

POWER FINISHING SANDER or HAND SANDING BLOCK

ROUTER

STRAIGHT ROUTER BIT – $\frac{1}{4}$in (6mm)

V-CUTTING ROUTER BIT

MARKING GAUGE

DRILL STAND

BRAD-POINT BIT – $\frac{3}{8}$in (10mm)

FLAT BIT – 1in (25mm)

SMOOTHING PLANE

Shelves

Mark off the shelf spacings at 8in (200mm) centers down the backboard (fig. 1). Mark horizontal lines across the width of the board at these points.

Using a router and a straight bit, rout a dado at each marked position $\frac{3}{8}$in (10mm) deep and to the thickness of the shelf (fig. 2, above). Alternatively, cut the dados for the shelves using a back saw, and remove the waste with a chisel.

Cut the shelves to length, sand smooth, and round over the corners. Center each shelf in position, and drill and countersink from the back of the backboard. Apply adhesive to a groove, and fit a shelf with three $1\frac{1}{2}$in (38mm) No. 8 woodscrews (fig. 2, below). Repeat for other shelves.

Paint or finish as required.

Rails

Mark off the rail spacings at 8in (200mm) centers down the backboard (fig. 1). Mark across the width of the board. At these positions, rout across the board using a V-cutting bit or cut with a back saw (fig. 3, above). The grooves allow the rails to locate into the backboard.

Cut the dowels to length. Drill and countersink from the back of the backboard into each rail to take three $1\frac{1}{2}$in (38mm) No. 8 screws (fig. 3, below). Apply adhesive to the grooves in the backboard, center the dowel rails one at a time, and screw the rails in place.

Paint or finish as required.

Pegs

Cut the seven pegs from the hardwood dowel to length (fig. 1). They start at 12in (about 304mm) and decrease by $1\frac{1}{2}$in (38mm) each time down to 3in (about 76mm), so that their ends form a straight, sloping line after fastening.

Mark off the peg spacings down the backboard (fig. 1), and, with a marking gauge, mark a vertical line centrally down the backboard to give the drilling positions.

In order to prevent items from sliding down the pegs, rout a shallow half-round groove across what will be the upper side of each peg, 1in (25mm) from the ends (fig. 4). It is best to use a router for this, but you can also use a drill; if a drill is used, clamp two pegs together and drill between them, 1in (25mm) from the end, to form a groove in each.

Drill 1in (25mm) diameter holes into the backboards from the front, at an angle of about 63 degrees, until the point of the drill bit just emerges through the back of the board. There are two ways of angling the pegs accurately: either the drill can be held upright in a drill stand and the backboard held at a 63 degree angle on a specially cut wedge; or the drill can be held in place at a 63 degree angle using a portable drill guide tool accessory available from tool shops.

Apply adhesive to the holes and push in the dowels in the correct order (fig. 1) until they are stopped by the back of the holes. When the glue has set, plane the parts of the pegs protruding at the back of the board so they are flush.

Paint or finish as required.

Installing the Units

Drill and countersink at the top and bottom of the backboards, 2in (50mm) in from the ends and screw and anchor securely to the wall (*see* **Techniques, page 120**), ensuring that the backboard is vertical.

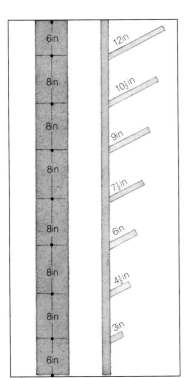

ASSEMBLY

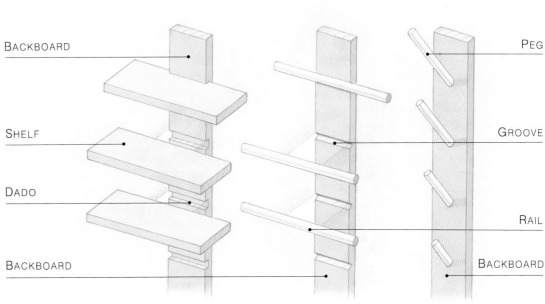

BACKBOARD

SHELF

DADO

BACKBOARD

PEG

GROOVE

RAIL

BACKBOARD

1 Spacings on the Backboard
Left: Mark length of backboard as indicated. *Right:* Cut peg dowels to decrease by 1½in (38mm) each time.

2 Fitting the Shelves
Rout or cut dados for the shelves at marked positions. Glue and screw in place from back of board.

3 Fitting the Rails
Rout or cut V-shaped grooves at marked positions. Glue and screw rails in place from back of board.

4 Fitting the Pegs
Above left: Rout shallow grooves across tops of pegs, 1in (25mm) from front. *Below left:* Position the pegs in the backboard, angled upward at 63 degrees. *Right:* Glue pegs in place; plane ends flush with back of board.

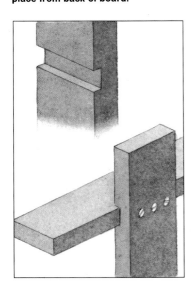

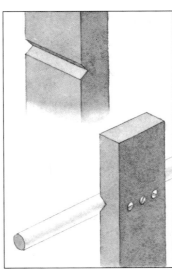

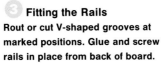

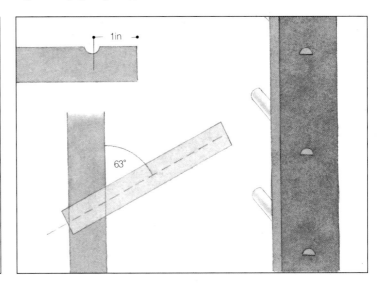

CHILD'S FOUR-POSTER BED

Your child can be a prince or princess every night in this bed. It consists of a simple lumber framework with $\frac{3}{4} \times 4$in (18×100mm) tongue-and-groove and V-jointed matching pine cladding, and a medium-density fiberboard (MDF) base for the mattress to rest on. Make the bed to fit the mattress.

The four corner posts are 3×3in (75×75mm) smooth 4 sides (S4S) softwood, 60in (1500mm) long. The framing at the base is $1\frac{1}{2}$in $\times 2$in (38×50mm) S4S lumber (fig. 1). For a really professional job this should be rabbeted into the corner posts by 1in (25mm) as shown, although it is possible simply to butt join the pieces using screw-on plastic block connectors used for joining wood at right angles.

At the sides and foot of the bed, the framing timbers are aligned with the inside faces of the corner posts to allow for the lumber cladding to be fixed on the sides and end of the bed (fig. 2). At the head end, the framing timbers are aligned with the outside faces of the posts so the cladding faces inward (fig. 3).

The cladding is glued and nailed to the lumber framing. On the head and foot ends of the bed, the top edge of the cladding is nailed to a 1×2in (25×50mm) batten which is fitted narrow edge upward between the corner posts.

The mattress support board is $\frac{3}{4}$in (18mm) thick MDF which sits on the top framing battens and a support strip screwed to the headboard. Supported along all four edges, the board for a single-bed mattress will not need additional support across the middle. To give access to the storage area under the mattress, cut an opening about 24×36in (600×900mm) in the center of the mattress support board. Frame the underside of the opening with 1×2in (25×50mm) lumber and replace the cut-out section after drilling a 1in (25mm) diameter hole in it as a finger pull for lifting it. Drill additional 1in (25mm) holes in the support board to air the mattress.

To complete the effect, fit 1×2in (25×50mm) battens between the corner posts at the top, to which decorations can be fitted.

1 General Construction of the Frame
Left: The frame consists of lengths of $1\frac{1}{2} \times 2$in (38×50mm) S4S joined to corner posts and then clad with tongue-and-groove boarding. *Right:* Ideally, the framing timbers should be housed into the corner posts.

2 Side Detail
Nail tongue-and-groove boards to the outside of the frame. Top length acts as mattress support.

3 Rear View of Headboard
At the head of the bed, cladding is nailed inside the frame; a third batten is fitted to support top edge.

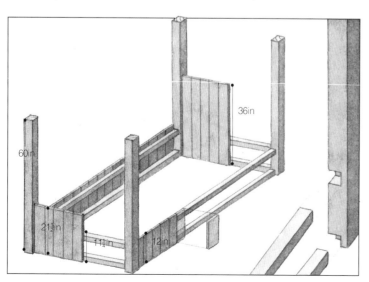

60in

36in

$21\frac{1}{2}$in

$11\frac{1}{2}$in

12in

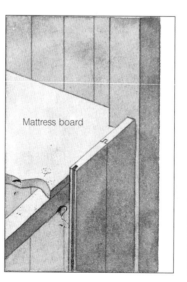

Mattress board

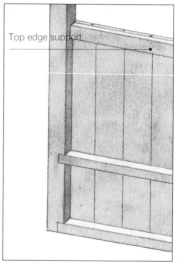

Top edge support

LOW-LEVEL SHELVES

Low-level shelving with invisible fixing supports can look most attractive in a wide alcove in a child's room, especially when it matches the flooring as shown here. In our example solid wood shelving is used, but the same effect can be achieved at considerably less cost by constructing hollow box-section shelving. In either case, the method of fitting to the back wall is the same.

In our photograph, the shelves are $1\frac{1}{2}$in (38mm) thick, 9in (230mm) deep and span the width of the alcove. If solid lumber can be obtained in suitable lengths, it is simply carefully planed and sanded smooth. If the depth you require is not available, two or more pieces can be glued together using biscuit joints or dowel joints along the length of the pieces of lumber to reinforce the join (fig. 1). The wood is clamped together until the glue has set, and then the shelf is planed and sanded smooth.

Box-section shelves are made by nailing top and bottom panels of $\frac{1}{4}$in (6mm) thick plywood over a framework of 1 × 1in (25 × 25mm)

battens; the back batten is recessed 1in (25mm) to take a support batten fixed to the wall (fig. 2). The shelves are edged with $\frac{5}{8} \times 1\frac{1}{2}$in (16 × 38mm) lumber battens mitered at the corners to give a neat finish and a solid appearance. By using $1\frac{1}{2}$in (38mm) wide edging on a $1\frac{3}{8}$in (37mm) thick shelf, you can sand down the edge to give an excellent

finish, and if the edging matches the lumber used to veneer the plywood, the result will be a box shelf that looks almost like solid wood.

The shelves are fitted invisibly to the back wall with $\frac{1}{2}$in (12mm) thick steel rods. These should be set 3in (75mm) into predrilled holes in the wall and should pass into matching holes in the shelves. In the case of a

solid shelf these should be drilled at least 6in (150mm) deep. With a hollow shelf the rods pass through a 1in (25mm) square support batten fixed to the wall. They must still be 3in (75mm) in the wall itself, and in the shelf should be set as deep as the front batten. Packing pieces about $\frac{1}{4}$in (6mm) thick hold the shelves level at the front.

① Making a Deep Solid Shelf
For a deeper shelf, join two widths using biscuit joints (above) or dowel joints (below).

② Making a Box-section Shelf
A box-section shelf can be made using veneered plywood over wood battens and edged with solid wood.

③ Basic Assembly and Fitting of a Box-section Shelf
Above: **The basic framework is nailed together with space left at the back for a support batten to be screwed to the wall.** ***Below:*** **Cross section shows steel rods set into the shelf with 3in (75mm) protruding into the wall.**

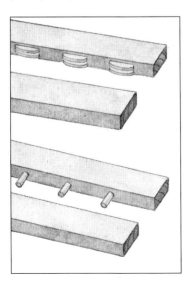

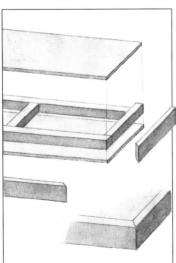

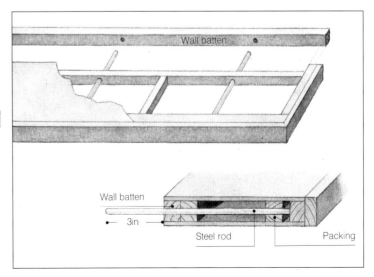

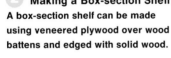

PART 2

PLAYROOMS

Play, in all its forms, is a vital element in a child's development. Children play to develop and test their skills, to explore their imaginations, to act out different roles, to learn how to share toys and games, and to get along together.

Play can be messy, noisy, and boisterous; it may well require supervision. Children learn by copying what their parents do and need access to the adult world to develop; very young children need a watchful eye until they can negotiate the world safely. But there are equally times when children need to shut the door behind them and get on with their own private world of make-believe. And adults too need to feel that some corner of the house is not dominated by children and their toys.

The element of magical transformation – making something out of nothing – can form the basis of a child's most memorable hours of play. A sheet thrown over a table and painted to look like a house, old cardboard boxes turned into robots or monsters, a castle constructed of upturned chairs and a pile of blankets will be remembered long after the plastic toy advertised on television has been broken and discarded.

PLAYROOMS

PLAYROOM STORAGE

Low-level units are accessible and adaptable without being obtrusive (above). The complete storage wall (above right) incorporates rows of drawers, cupboards with doors for hiding clutter, and a configuration of shelving to suit every requirement from storing books, records, and games to displaying treasured possessions. A ladder on wheels securely anchored to a rail provides access to the topmost compartments.

The fluid and varied nature of children's play means that no parents can equip a "playroom" and reasonably expect their children to spend most of their time there. A series of play areas in the house is a more realistic and practical proposition; equally there should be rooms which remain firmly designated for grown-ups. For most children, their bedroom will also be the place where they play. Really messy activities, such as painting and model-making, are often best tackled in the kitchen (when space permits), where surfaces are more easily cleaned. For many households with young children, it may well be worth turning a separate dining room into a family room or play area, at least in the early years when children need more supervision. More permanent solutions include converting an attic or fitting out a basement. Children love unusual, quirky spaces – under the eaves or an alcove beneath the stairs can be magical hiding and playing places.

EQUIPMENT AND FURNISHING

In their earlier years, children spend a great deal of time playing on the floor. Flooring in any play area needs to be especially practical and hard-wearing, as well as comfortable. Restricting certain types of particularly messy activity to areas where spills can be easily mopped up can help to prolong the life of a playroom carpet or rug. And because many games demand a lot of floor area, tables, chairs and other pieces of play equipment which can be packed away, folded up, or stacked add flexibility to a room. Stacking stools, folding chairs, and painting easels that fold away are all good, versatile, and space-saving playroom items.

Although it is best to avoid too much in the way of miniaturized furniture, child-sized table and chairs are indispensable for painting, drawing, and other creative pursuits, as well as dolls' tea parties, games of shop-keeping, and play

school. When your child eventually outgrows this set of furniture, it will be time to provide a proper desk or table for homework and quiet study. A good chair that supports the back well is essential. Old school desks can also be revamped with a coat of paint.

As with furniture, any wall decoration which is tied specifically to one age group will need to be changed before too long, so it is best to choose a style that will suit children of different ages. Friezes and borders are extremely popular. There is now a wide range of paper borders available, featuring alphabets, animals, trains, and a host of other appropriate designs. The same effect can be achieved by stenciling designs onto the wall in horizontal bands or by using templates to create a simple row of figures, and the advantage of this approach is that you can paint over the design very quickly and easily when your child has outgrown the decoration or wants a change.

Wallpaper designed for children, patterned with everything from nursery-style ducks and rabbits to comic book-style airplanes, is also widely available, though it is usually horrible. Less specific patterns, such as more abstract geometric shapes, have a longer life, however. Alternatively, special paint effects can be used to create a uniquely patterned wall. Sponges, rags, and stipple brushes can be used to make speckled and mottled paint finishes that are quick and easy to apply and that have a lively surface appeal and depth of interest.

STORAGE AND DISPLAY

Crunching across a floor littered with small plastic bricks and the debris of an afternoon's riotous play is an all-too-familiar experience for most parents. Children and clutter seem indivisible; to the bounty of birthdays and Christmases will be added mounting collections of "precious" objects which must on no

PLAYING PLACES

The nature of the play area itself can provide a springboard for the imagination, prompting all manner of games and play activities. Play space underneath projecting platform bedrooms has an appealing enclosed feeling like a den or hideout, where children can retreat to escape the watchful eyes of grown-ups (above left). A wall painted to look like the Three Bears' cottage makes a vivid backdrop for games of make-believe (above).

PLAYROOMS

DOLL'S HOUSE

The miniaturized world of the doll's house has fascinated children for generations. Making and furnishing such a house down to the last detail can be as absorbing a pastime for a parent as it is for a child (left and above). And the greater the attention to detail you pay in furnishing and decorating the interior of a doll's house, the more time and enjoyment your children will derive from playing with it.

WORK TABLES

To encourage children's creativity you don't necessarily need a full-scale studio, but a good work table, an easel, and storage boxes and drawers to keep materials in order are invaluable (left). Young children, too, need somewhere to sit and paint, such as this set of table and chairs with "crayon" legs (below).

account be thrown out. But accumulating is one thing, tidying up quite another. Good storage plays a vital role in bringing order out of your children's chaos and helping to teach them to put things away.

For children, toys, rather than books, do furnish a room. Storage which incorporates some means of display enables children to enjoy the feeling of being surrounded by their favorite things. Systems of adjustable shelves allow books and toys to be arranged on view, well within reach, with games requiring adult supervision or breakable possessions on a higher level. Wall hooks or pegs can be used for hanging up puppets or kites beyond the grasp of small siblings. And it is important to make provision for dis-

playing the latest examples of your children's work. A pinboard or pegboard allows you to rotate pictures easily. For older children you might put up a calendar, world map, or museum posters.

To keep the clutter under control, labeled wire baskets or stacking crates can be used to organize and keep separate games or toys with many tiny components. Containers with divisions, such as tool boxes, make good places for crayons, paints, or craft supplies. A wicker hamper or old school trunk is ideal for storing dressing-up clothes. And a large basket or blanket box with a hinged safety lid makes a good all-purpose toy box into which things can be hurled out of sight at the end of the day's play.

FINISHING TOUCHES

However you tackle the basic features of your child's room, it is the details and finishing touches that will bring it to life. Such features as height charts, name plates, your child's own framed drawings or paintings hung on the wall, or a row of favorite toys will all help make a room a special and meaningful place for a child. And there should always be a reasonable amount of space – a shelf, table top, or top of a chest of drawers, for instance – for those much-loved shrine-like collections of bits and pieces that all children seem to take such pleasure in accumulating and that are an important part of their learning process.

PLAYROOMS

PLAYING AWAY

If you have the space, a playroom is the ideal place for children to let their imaginations and creativity run loose. The playroom here is equipped with the Painting Table and Doll's House projects contained in this book, as well as some quick and effective decorating ideas. The brightly patterned screen on the left of the main picture is painted with blackboard paint on the other side to allow children to chalk away to their hearts' content (above). A striking and surprisingly simple effect is created by painting a "picture frame" on the wall, inside of which a painted bowl is stacked high with glued-on papier mâché fruit.

DOLL'S HOUSE

The doll's house has always been a popular toy, and it is easy to understand why. The first dolls' houses were elaborate curios, intricate architectural models with highly detailed interiors. But, ever since the eighteenth century, there have also been dolls' houses for children to play with and exercise their own creativity. A house in miniature gives children the opportunity to invent a whole world, and there is the added fascination of making or collecting pieces to furnish the rooms.

Rather reminiscent of a Scottish house, with its pedimented roof and blockwork framing the door, this design is a very simple box construction, with a hinged front panel. The four rooms inside are visible through cut-out windows. A strip of molding and pediment shape elegantly trim the top; thin plywood scored to resemble large blocks is stuck around the door. The basic material is MDF (medium-density fiberboard), which is easy to cut and quick to decorate.

If you already have a collection of doll's house furniture, the dimensions of the house could be altered to make rooms of suitable proportions. And decoration, inside and out, can be as elaborate as you like. The paint finish for the outside of the house in this example consists of a sandy base color with shoe polish wiped over the top to give a textured look.

The finished house is handsome enough to sit in the living room. Every child should have one!

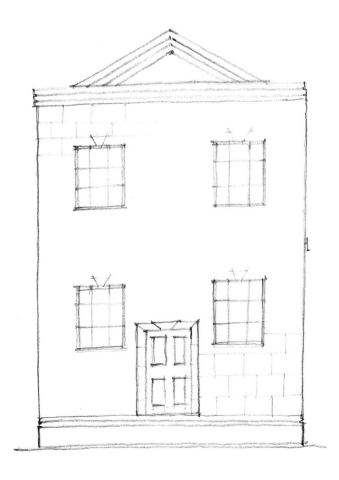

DOLL'S HOUSE

MATERIALS

Part	Quantity	Material	Length
CARCASS			
TOP	1	$\frac{5}{8}$in (15mm) MDF	$12\frac{5}{8} \times 25\frac{1}{2}$in (321 × 650mm)
BASE	1	As above	$13\frac{1}{8} \times 25\frac{1}{2}$in (335 × 650mm)
SIDE	2	As above	$12\frac{5}{8} \times 27\frac{3}{4}$in (321 × 705mm)
CENTRAL PARTITION	1	As above	$12\frac{1}{2} \times 27\frac{3}{8}$in (316 × 695mm)
SHELF	2	As above	$12\frac{1}{4} \times 12\frac{1}{2}$in (312 × 316mm)
BACK	1	$\frac{1}{8}$in (4mm) MDF or plywood or hardboard	$25\frac{1}{4} \times 27\frac{3}{4}$in (640 × 705mm)
DOOR PANEL	1	$\frac{1}{2}$in (12mm) MDF	$25\frac{1}{2} \times 26$in (650 × 660mm)
PLINTH			
PLINTH FRONT	1	$\frac{3}{4}$in (18mm) MDF	$3 \times 26\frac{3}{8}$in (75 × 670mm)
PLINTH BACK	1	As above	3×25in (75 × 634mm)
PLINTH SIDE	2	As above	$3 \times 13\frac{1}{2}$in (75 × 345mm)
DETAILING			
FRONT MOLDING	1	$\frac{5}{8}$in (15mm) MDF	$1\frac{1}{2} \times 26\frac{3}{4}$in (40 × 680mm)
SIDE MOLDING	2	As above	Cut 2 from $1\frac{1}{2} \times 26\frac{3}{4}$in (40 × 680mm)
TOP MOLDING	2	As above	$1\frac{1}{2} \times 19\frac{5}{8}$in (40 × 500mm)
TOP TRIANGLE	1	$\frac{1}{8}$in (4mm) MDF	$3\frac{5}{8} \times 17\frac{1}{2}$in (90 × 445mm)
DOOR STOP	2	$\frac{5}{8}$in (15mm) MDF	$1\frac{3}{8} \times 25\frac{1}{2}$in (35 × 650mm)
DOOR (imitation)	1	$\frac{1}{16}$in (2mm) MDF	3×8in (75 × 200mm)
GLAZING BAR (vertical)	4	$\frac{1}{4} \times \frac{1}{4}$in (6 × 6mm) balsa-wood	$6\frac{1}{2}$in (165mm)
GLAZING BAR (horizontal)	8	As above	5in (125mm)

TOOLS

ROUTER
SET OF CHISELS
BACK SAW
TACK HAMMER
NAILSET
FILLING KNIFE
SCREWDRIVER
ADJUSTABLE BEVEL
DRILL (hand or power)
SABER SAW or COMPASS SAW
DRILL BIT – approximately $\frac{1}{8}$in (3mm) to drill pilot holes

A traditional doll's house is a wonderful toy that any child lucky enough to own will treasure and enjoy for endless hours of make-believe. This simple yet classic model is easy to construct with the help of a router. The advantage of its design is its adaptability – you can scale its dimensions up or down to tailor them to specific requirements. When constructing a doll's house it is important to base the scale on what is to be placed inside it, so that the rooms are built in correct proportion to furniture, furnishings, or figures of a specific size.

The house is built almost totally of medium-density fiberboard (MDF). A small amount of balsa-wood provides the glazing bars, and plywood or hardboard may be used instead of MDF for the back.

Paper or paint the walls as you wish. You can either improvise or visit specialty shops for ready-made furniture and accessories.

MAIN SECTION

Cut out all the components of the main section – the top, base, sides, central partition, shelves, and back.

Rout a rabbet $\frac{5}{8}$in (15mm) wide and $\frac{3}{8}$in (10mm) deep along the two side edges of the top panel from front to back (fig. 1, above).

Cut rabbets of the same dimensions in the two side edges of the base, but stop $\frac{5}{8}$in (15mm) from the front to allow the base to protrude (fig. 1, below). Chisel the corners of the rabbets square.

1 Rabbeting the Main Carcass
Above: Rout $\frac{3}{8} \times \frac{5}{8}$in (10 × 15mm) rabbets along top panel. *Below:* Rabbets along base stop short.

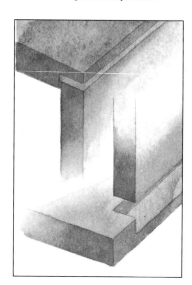

2 Top and Base Dados
Cut $\frac{1}{4} \times \frac{5}{8}$in (5 × 15mm) dados across center of top and base panels, stopping short in base.

DOLL'S HOUSE ASSEMBLY

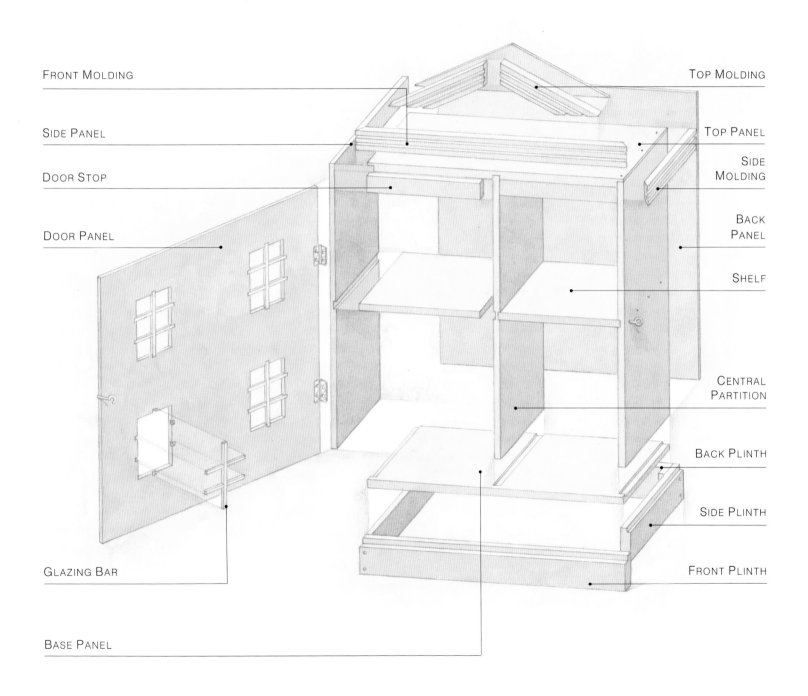

FRONT MOLDING

SIDE PANEL

DOOR STOP

DOOR PANEL

GLAZING BAR

BASE PANEL

TOP MOLDING

TOP PANEL

SIDE MOLDING

BACK PANEL

SHELF

CENTRAL PARTITION

BACK PLINTH

SIDE PLINTH

FRONT PLINTH

DOLL'S HOUSE

CUTTING THE DADOS

Across the center of the top and the sides and across the center of both sides of the central partition, cut $\frac{1}{4} \times \frac{5}{8}$in (5 × 15mm) dados to accept the interior partitions. Cut a dado across the base but stop $\frac{5}{8}$in (15mm) short of the front, in line with the side edges (fig. 2, page 54 and fig. 1, page 56).

RABBETING BACK PANEL

Cut a rabbet into the back edges of the top, sides, and base for the back panel. This rabbet should be $\frac{3}{8}$in (10mm) wide and the thickness of the back panel — $\frac{1}{8}$in (4mm).

ASSEMBLING THE HOUSE

Glue and nail the top to the sides and then the base. Ensure all edges are flush and square. Slide the central partition in from the back and glue and nail it in place. Next, slide in the two shelves from the back of the main section and glue and nail them through the sides of the house. Finally, glue and nail the back panel in place (fig. 2). All the

nail heads should be driven below the surface with a nailset, covered with filler, and smoothed flush with the surface when dry.

PLINTH

Cut out the four sides of the plinth and glue and screw them together using two 1$\frac{1}{2}$in (38mm) No. 6 screws at each joint. The sides fit behind the front and on either side of the back. Glue a $\frac{3}{4}$in (18mm) offcut of MDF into each corner to strengthen the joints. The offcuts should be flush with, or slightly below, the plinth top (fig. 3). Cut a decorative rabbet $\frac{1}{4} \times \frac{1}{4}$in (6mm × 6mm) into the top outside edge of the plinth front.

Screw the plinth to the base using 2in (50mm) angle brackets – two at the front and two at the back.

FITTING THE DOOR STOPS

Cut two lengths of $\frac{5}{8}$in (15mm) MDF for the door stops. Screw these in position to the underside of the top panel on either side of the central partition using glue and 1in (25mm) No. 6 screws (see **Doll's House Assembly, page 55**).

MOLDINGS

Cut all the moldings (front, side, and top) roughly to length, then use the router to cut two decorative $\frac{1}{4} \times \frac{1}{4}$in (6 × 6mm) grooves along their length (fig. 4). Cut miters for the corners of the front and side moldings, then glue and nail them in place, flush with the top (fig. 5).

Cut out the triangle for the top decoration from a piece of $\frac{1}{8}$in (4mm) MDF. The two top moldings must be angled at their base (where they meet the top of the house) and mitered to meet each other at the apex. Use an adjustable bevel to mark the angles, then glue and nail them onto the triangular piece of MDF, flush with the edges and so that the grooves meet exactly.

Using a small drill bit, drill pilot holes into the front triangular molding and nail in position through the molding and into the roof. Glue an offcut of MDF to the back of the triangle and the top of the house to hold the triangle in place. Punch all the nail heads below the surface and fill.

WINDOWS

Cut out the door panel and mark the outlines of the windows on it: ours measure 4$\frac{1}{2}$ × 6in (110 × 150mm). Cut out the window openings using a saber saw, a compass saw (drill a starter hole in the corner of each window first), or a router.

GLAZING BARS

Balsa-wood, obtainable from model shops, is ideal for the glazing bars. For each window, cut one vertical and two horizontal bars. Each should be $\frac{1}{2}$in (15mm) longer than the length and width of the window opening – in this case, 6$\frac{1}{2}$in (165mm) and 5in (125mm). Use a fine saw and a tiny chisel to cut cross-lap joints halfway across the horizontal bars and one-third and two-thirds of the way down the vertical bars (fig. 6). Glue the pieces together. Mark off the positions of the glazing bars around the edges of the inside faces of the window openings. Use a tiny chisel to cut out $\frac{1}{4} \times \frac{1}{4}$in (6 × 6mm) notches. Glue the assembled bars in position.

---

1 Central Partition Dados
Cut $\frac{1}{4} \times \frac{5}{8}$in (5 × 15mm) dados for interior partitions across center of both sides of central panel.

2 Adding the Back Panel
The back panel fits into $\frac{1}{8} \times \frac{3}{8}$in (4 × 10mm) rabbets cut in the back edges of the top, sides and base.

3 Assembling the Base Plinth
Above: Glue and screw plinth together, strengthening corners with MDF scraps. *Below left* Cut a $\frac{1}{4} \times \frac{1}{4}$in (6 × 6mm) rabbet in top edge of plinth front. *Below right:* Use angle brackets to screw plinth up into base.

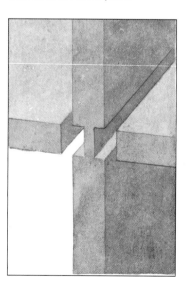

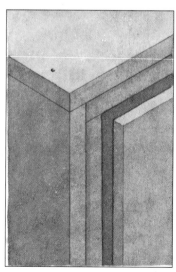

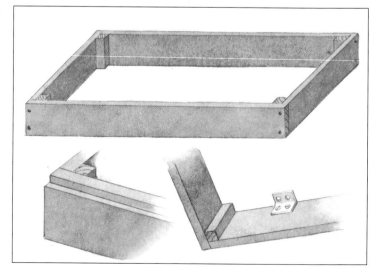

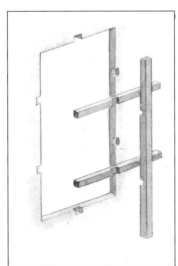

4 **Routing the Moldings**
Cut moldings for the front, sides, and top; rout out two $\frac{1}{4} \times \frac{1}{4}$in (6 × 6mm) grooves along their lengths.

5 **Adding the Moldings**
Cut miters in the ends where front and side moldings meet. Glue and nail them flush with top of carcass.

6 **Fitting the Glazing Bars**
Cut half-lap joints to join horizontal and vertical bars. Glue the bars into notches around window edges.

FINISHING OFF

Make a false front door from an offcut of MDF and glue it in place on the front of the door panel. Hang the door panel using two butt hinges and fit a hook-and-eye catch on the other side of the house.

You can paint the house in various ways: for example, latex for the walls, and undercoat and gloss to pick out the door, windows, and moldings. The exterior finish shown here is achieved by painting the body with a base color of yellow latex. When this has dried, roughly pencil in the brickwork. Finally, rub a small amount of shoe polish gently over the surface. Use an artist's paintbrush around delicate areas such as the window frames. Protect the paint effect with a topcoat of clear varnish.

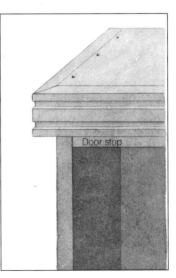

Door stop

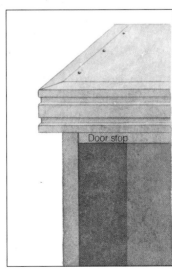

PAINTING TABLE

Although the kitchen table may be a practical place for children to draw and paint, it is much better if they have a table scaled to their own size, where they can also keep crayons, brushes, and a supply of paper permanently at hand. From a surprisingly early age children enjoy making pictures, even if at the beginning these are no more than the briefest of scribbles. A painting table will encourage them to explore their creative instincts.

No more than about half a day's work, this simple pine table consists of a framework that is glued and screwed or doweled together. It is topped with a hinged lid made of melamine-faced board to enable splashes and spills to be wiped away easily. The lid covers a storage space deep enough to take boxes of crayons and other drawing and painting materials. Alternatively, the top can be screwed down and the base omitted.

Children can go through a great deal of paper. At one side of the table, a dowel drops in place and can be used to hold a roll of lining paper, a versatile and cheap way of meeting children's paper needs; you can tear off individual sheets or unroll a long length for murals or banners. At the other side of the table, there is a place to keep plastic jars filled with poster paints or water, which helps to reduce mess and accidental spills.

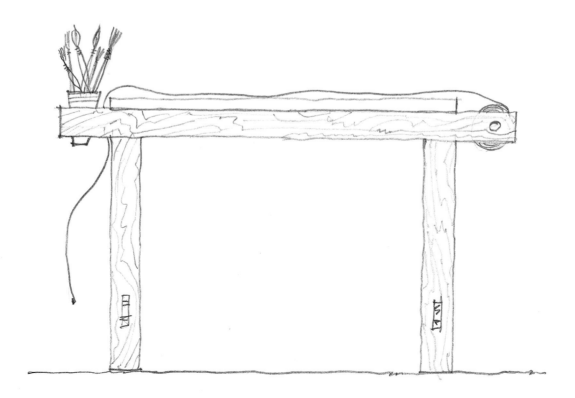

PAINTING TABLE

PRIDE OF PLACE

When they've finished painting, children need a means to display their work. We painted a board with a church and some houses, cut it out, and stuck a magnetic strip across the bottom to hold the paintings.

Every child loves to paint. It's the perfect outlet for fun, imagination, education, and creativity. When a child has a paintbrush, lovely colors, and water with which to experiment, it is clearly time to leave self-expression free to develop. But this cannot be achieved in a restrictive atmosphere, and finding that ideal somewhere for such a messy activity is not always easy.

The understandable and necessary concern for the protection of furniture and furnishings can be obviated, however, with this simple, functional painting table. It provides an activity center combined with storage for materials so that setting up and clearing away takes only a minute or two.

The design of this table is based on a standard roll of wall lining-paper which can be obtained at any decorating shop. It is a cheap, white paper normally pasted onto walls but which provides a large amount of paper ideal for painting on. The roll is stored on a dowel at one end of the table and can be pulled across the top to provide a continuous clean painting surface as required. The used paper is fed through a small gap at the other end of the table. Circular holes are cut in a shelf at one end of the table to provide safe storage for paint and water containers.

The table top is made from melamine-faced chipboard, so it has a wipe-clean surface. Although the top could be permanently screwed down, with a little more effort a base can be added and the top hinged so that it can be raised to give access to a convenient storage area for painting materials beneath it.

PAINTING TABLE ASSEMBLY

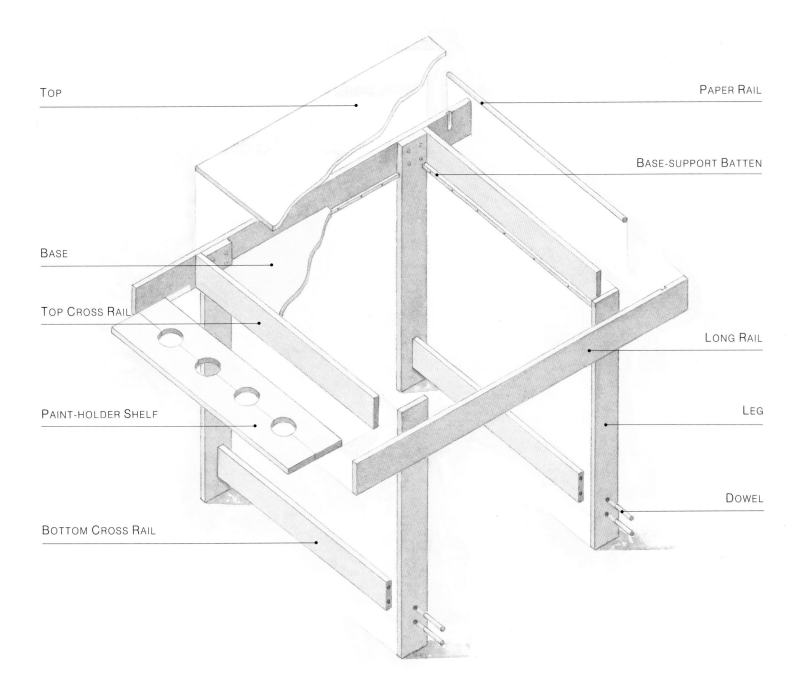

TOP

PAPER RAIL

BASE-SUPPORT BATTEN

BASE

TOP CROSS RAIL

LONG RAIL

PAINT-HOLDER SHELF

LEG

DOWEL

BOTTOM CROSS RAIL

PAINTING TABLE

CONSTRUCTION

Cut the top rails and legs to length. Round over the ends of the long rails to reduce impact injuries. Cut the paint-holder rails and join them with adhesive; clamp and leave to dry.

TOP FRAME

On the two long rails, mark the positions of the center lines of the top cross rails. These will be 6in (150mm) in from the paint-holder end and $4\frac{1}{2}$in (110mm) in from the other end. Square the marks around onto the opposite faces of the long rails.

Into each of the four marked center lines, drill three equally spaced holes to accept 2in (50mm) No. 8 screws. Countersink each hole so that the screw heads will be flush with the surface (*see* **Techniques, page 120**). Glue and screw the long rails to the ends of the top cross rails, ensuring that they are exactly square at the points where they join (fig. 1). Clamp the joints together while the glue dries.

LEGS

The legs should be fitted tight into the inside corners of the frame to ensure rigidity. Each leg is glued and screwed from inside the frame using four $1\frac{1}{2}$in (38mm) No. 8 screws (fig. 2). Drill and countersink the holes through the legs and into the long rails, ensuring that their top edges are flush with the top of the frame.

BOTTOM CROSS RAILS

Measure for and cut the bottom cross rails to length. The top edge of each rail should be 6in (150mm) up from the bottom of each leg. Mark a line and square around onto the opposite face and mark off two equally spaced dowel positions. Clamp one rail accurately centered in position between two legs, then drill $\frac{1}{2}$in (12mm) diameter, 3in (75mm) deep holes through the legs and into the rail. Repeat for the other bottom cross rail.

Cut and prepare eight $\frac{1}{2}$in (12mm) diameter dowels, $3\frac{1}{4}$in (80mm) long. Score thin grooves along the length of each dowel.

HINGED TABLE TOP

The simple addition of hinges to the table top and a base beneath creates a space in which paints, pencils, and crayons can be stored. The paint-holder shelf prevents jars of paint from tipping over.

① Constructing the Top Frame
Mark on the long rails the positions of the top cross rails so they are 6in (150mm) in from one end and $4\frac{1}{2}$in (110mm) from the other. Glue and screw through the long rails into the ends of the top cross rails.

② Fitting the Legs
The legs are glued and screwed tightly and squarely into the inside corners of the top frame.

③ Bottom Cross Rails
Position the cross rails between the legs, 6in (150mm) up from the bottom. Drill and dowel in place.

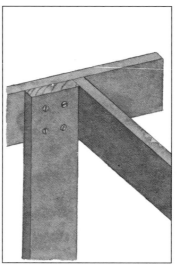

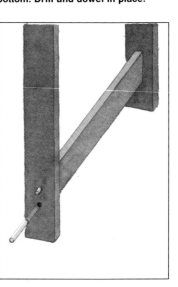

Apply aliphatic resin to each hole, then hammer home the dowels leaving the ends protruding (fig. 3). Leave the clamps in place until the adhesive has set, then saw off the protruding dowel for a flush finish.

PAINT-HOLDER SHELF

The number and diameter of holes is optional and will be determined by the size of the jars or other containers used. Here we used four equally spaced 2in (50mm) diameter holes (fig. 4). They can be cut using an expansive bit, a hole saw, a saber saw or a compass saw (see **Techniques, page 118**).

Position the shelf between the long rails, flush with their undersides and ends. You should leave a small gap between the innermost edge of the paintholder shelf and the outside face of the top cross rail for the paper to feed through – if the gap is not wide enough, plane a little off the edge of the shelf.

Drill four countersunk holes in the edge of each long rail and fit the shelf in place using 2in (50mm) No. 8 screws (fig. 5).

PAPER RAIL

At the opposite end of the table, fit the dowel that holds the roll of paper. This simply rests in slots cut centrally into the protruding ends of the long rails (fig. 6). The slots are $\frac{1}{2}$in (12mm) wide and 1in (25mm) deep. Ensure the two slots are aligned with careful marking before drilling. Drill a hole at the base of the slot, then saw down the sides with a back saw. Pare out the waste of each slot with a chisel. Cut the dowel long enough to fit snugly in position, without it being too tight.

TABLE TOP

The top should be cut to fit flush with the outside edges of the long rails and cross rails. Measure the exact dimensions before cutting. It is a good idea to ask the supplier to cut this to size for you, since melamine-faced board sometimes splinters along the cut. The exposed, sawn edges of the top should be covered with iron-on edging strip which is readily available where you buy your melamine-faced particleboard.

If you want a fixed top, secure it to the cross rail using 2in (50mm) angle brackets screwed to the inside of the top frame and the underside of the table top – two on each side will give a secure fastening.

For a hinged top, use two 3in (75mm) hinges – flush hinges are easiest to fit (see **Techniques, page 122**). For safety, fit a support stay to hold the top firmly in position when it is raised up.

BASE

Fit this only if you hinge the top. Cut four lengths of $\frac{3}{8} \times \frac{3}{8}$in (9 × 9mm) hardwood for the base supports. Glue and pin them flush with the bottom edges of the rails (fig. 7).

The base should be cut to fit the inside dimensions of the long rails and cross rails, so measure before cutting. Use an offcut from one of the 1 × 3in (25 × 75mm) legs as a template for the corner notches. Dab adhesive onto the supports to hold the base in position.

Make sure the wood is free from splinters, then paint, stain, or varnish according to the finish you want.

④ Paint-holder Shelf
Join two lengths of 1 × 3in (25 × 75mm) S4S edge-on. Cut holes to fit the paint jar size.

⑤ Fitting Paint-holder Shelf
Position the shelf between the long rails, flush with the undersides and ends. Screw in place.

⑥ Fitting the Paper Rail
Cut slots on the inside faces of the long rails and rest a length of $\frac{1}{2}$in (12mm) dowel in place.

⑦ Adding a Base
The optional base is notched at the corners and rests on battens nailed to the long and top cross rails.

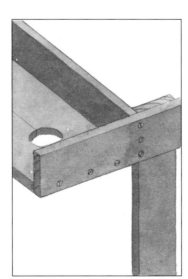

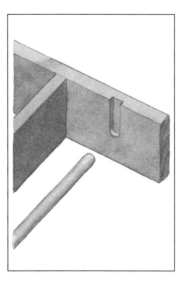

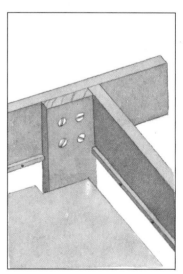

Swing-door Wardrobe

As with the Storage House on page 32, this design uses play as a means of encouraging children to look after their own belongings. Either as a free-standing unit or fitted into an alcove, the simple box framework is designed to accommodate hanging space for clothes on one side and a washbasin (optional) on the other. Compartments above can take folded clothes, shoes, toys, and sports gear. The size of the system overall can be adapted to suit the space available.

Made of lumber core or MDF (medium-density fiberboard), the frame construction is quick and easy. A length of dowel serves as a clothes rail.

The play value comes in the decoration of the door, which swings on hinges to reveal a "kitchen" on one side and a clothes "shop" on the other. Playing at cooking and running a shop are perennial favorites; the vivid backgrounds provided by each side of the door lend an extra dimension to the make-believe.

Decorating the door need not be difficult. You can cut out a series of basic shapes or stencil outlines to give a degree of uniformity and then apply real food labels from food cans or packets on the "kitchen" side, or stick on cut-out wrapping paper to trim the clothes on the "shop" side. In the same way, the lid of the toy box, which can be lifted out and reversed, is simply painted with circles to make the rings of a play stove on one side and as a shop counter on the other.

SWING-DOOR WARDROBE ASSEMBLY

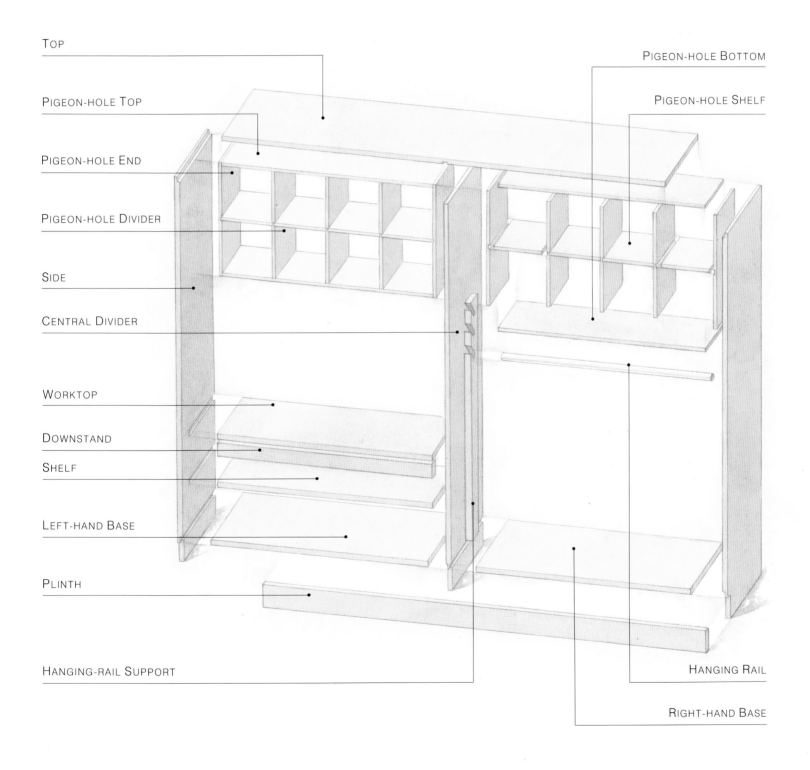

TOP

PIGEON-HOLE TOP

PIGEON-HOLE END

PIGEON-HOLE DIVIDER

SIDE

CENTRAL DIVIDER

WORKTOP

DOWNSTAND

SHELF

LEFT-HAND BASE

PLINTH

HANGING-RAIL SUPPORT

PIGEON-HOLE BOTTOM

PIGEON-HOLE SHELF

HANGING RAIL

RIGHT-HAND BASE

DOUBLE THE FUN

We painted the door with backdrops for playing against: when the right-hand side of the wardrobe is open, the door is painted to look like a shop (above); swing the door the other way, and a kitchen stacked with exotic ingredients is revealed (right).

Swing-door Wardrobe

Tools

WORKBENCH (fixed or portable)

STEEL MEASURING TAPE

TRY SQUARE

ADJUSTABLE BEVEL

SABER SAW

POWER DRILL

DRILL BITS – various for pilot holes

COUNTERSINK BIT

FLAT BIT – 1in (25mm)

CIRCULAR SAW or PANEL SAW

SMOOTHING PLANE (hand or power)

BELT SANDER or POWER FINISHING SANDER or HAND SANDING BLOCK

SCREWDRIVER

ROUTER

STRAIGHT-CUTTER BIT – $\frac{1}{2}$in (12mm) and $\frac{3}{4}$in (19mm)

Children will be able to keep their rooms tidy and have lots of fun with this combined wardrobe and shelving system, which doubles as a play area. It can be made to whatever width required, up to a maximum of 8ft (2.4m) (since the width of the swing-door panel must not exceed 48in [1220mm]). The unit has panels at each end, so it can be built as a free-standing unit against a wall, or it can be built wall-to-wall, or to fit into an alcove. Even if it is built-in, it should be built square as a free-standing unit and then pushed back into the alcove or between the side walls. If these walls are not true (exactly square), scribing fillets can be scribed to the wall to fill the gaps.

Whether the wardrobe is built-in or free-standing, for safety it must be fixed securely against the rear wall, as the door exerts a considerable pull away from the wall when it is swung from one side to the other. If you build the wardrobe to its maximum length, you will need 48in

Materials

Part	Quantity	Material	Length
Carcass			
SIDE	2	$\frac{3}{4}$in (18mm) lumber core or MDF	$21\frac{5}{8} \times 72$in (550 × 1830mm)
CENTRAL DIVIDER	1	As above	$21\frac{5}{8} \times 71\frac{1}{2}$in (550 × 1818mm)
TOP	1	As above	As required
BASE	2	As above	As required
WORKTOP	1	As above	As required
SHELF	1	As above	As required
PLINTH	1	As above	As required
Pigeon-hole Unit			
TOP	2	$\frac{1}{2}$in (12mm) lumber core or MDF	As required
BOTTOM	2	As above	As required
END	4	As above	As required
DIVIDER	6	As above	As required
SHELF	8	As above	As required
Wardrobe Section			
HANGING-RAIL SUPPORT	2	1 × 4in (25 × 100mm) S4S softwood	Cut to fit
HANGING RAIL	1	1in (25mm) diameter doweling	As above
DOWNSTAND	1	1 × 2in (25 × 50mm) S4S softwood	As above
DOOR	1	$\frac{3}{4}$in (18mm) lumber core	As above
FIXING BATTEN	2	1 × 1in (25 × 25mm) S4S softwood	72in (1830mm)
Toy Box			
FRONT	1	$\frac{3}{4}$in (18mm) lumber core or MDF	24 × 36in (600 × 900mm)
BACK	1	As above	As above
SIDE	2	As above	$22\frac{3}{4} \times 24$in (570 × 600mm)
BASE	1	$\frac{1}{4}$in (6mm) plywood	Cut to fit
BASE SUPPORT BATTEN	4	1 × 1in (25 × 25mm)	Cut to fit
LID SUPPORT BATTEN	3	As above	Cut to fit
LID	1	$\frac{1}{4}$in (6mm) plywood	$23\frac{1}{4} \times 36$in (590 × 900mm)

Also required: corner fixing blocks and scribing fillets; 4 screen hinges; 2 magnetic catches; angle brackets or fixing plates; 4 castors; silicone rubber mastic (for fixing washbasin).

(1220mm) of free space in front of the wardrobe for the door to swing open. If you do not have sufficient space, you can either scale down the length of the wardrobe, or you could cut the door panel down the middle and hinge the two pieces together with butt or folding door hinges so that they flap back on one another, needing only 24in (610mm) of free space in front.

The storage unit can be made from $\frac{3}{4}$in (18mm) MDF (medium-density fiberboard) or lumber core.

Lumber core is lighter and stronger than MDF; however, its exposed edges must be filled or covered with iron-on lipping. MDF is easy to cut and paint, but it is too heavy for the door panel. Size and weight dictate that assembly is done on site.

CONSTRUCTION

Measure for the width of the unit and allow about $1\frac{1}{2}$in (40mm) on either side if building wall-to-wall or into an alcove. This gap will be taken up by scribing fillets.

SIDES

Cut out the side panels and cut a $\frac{1}{4} \times \frac{3}{4}$in (6 × 18mm) rabbet along the top inside edge of each (fig. 1). Cut a $\frac{1}{4} \times \frac{3}{4}$in (6 × 18mm) dado on the inside for the base panel in each side panel (fig. 2). The bottom of the dado is positioned 3in (75mm) up from the bottom of the panel. Finally, cut a $\frac{3}{4} \times 3$in (18 × 75mm) notch in both side panels to take the plinth (fig. 2, below).

CENTRAL DIVIDER

Cut out the central divider. Cut a $\frac{1}{4} \times \frac{3}{4}$in (6 × 18mm) dado, 3in (75mm) up from the base on each side to take the base panels (fig. 3, above). Cut a $\frac{3}{4} \times 3$in (18 × 75mm) notch at the bottom to take the plinth (fig. 3, below).

TOP PANEL

Cut the top panel – this should be the overall width of the unit, less $\frac{15}{16}$in (about 24mm). On the underside, mark the center line across its width and cut out a $\frac{1}{4} \times \frac{3}{4}$in (6 × 18mm) central dado.

BASE PANELS

Cut out the two base panels. The length of each is the overall width of the unit divided in half, less $\frac{5}{8}$in (15mm) for each half. The width of each panel is $21\frac{5}{8}$in (550mm).

WORKTOP AND SHELF

These are both the same length as the base panels, but only $19\frac{3}{4}$in (500mm) wide. Cut $\frac{1}{4} \times \frac{3}{4}$in (6 × 18mm) dados for both these panels in the left-hand side panel and the left-hand side of the central divider (*see* **Swing-door Wardrobe**

Assembly, page 65). The worktop dado is $27\frac{1}{2}$in (700mm) up (from the bottom edge of the side panel to the bottom edge of the dado) and the shelf dado is $13\frac{3}{4}$in (350mm) up. The dados are stopped 2in (50mm) short of the front edge.

LEFT-HAND SIDE ASSEMBLY

Working from the outside of the left-hand side panel, drill and counter-sink through the three dados and the top rabbet for five screws in each joint. In the central divider, drill and countersink in the right-hand side through the dados in five places each time for the worktop, shelf, and bottom panel.

Lay the left-hand side panel on its back edge and glue and screw the worktop, shelf, and left-hand base panel into their respective dados (fig. 1, page 70).

Lay the central divider on its back edge, then offer it up in place. Glue and screw through the dados into the ends of the worktop, shelf, and base. Ensure that all screwheads are fully countersunk.

1 **Rabbeting Top of Side Panel**
Cut a $\frac{1}{4} \times \frac{3}{4}$in (6 × 18mm) rabbet along the top inside edge of the two side panels.

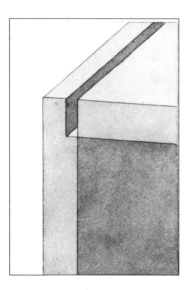

2 **Routing the Side Panel**
Above: On side panel inside face, cut a dado 3in (75mm) up from the bottom. *Below:* Cut notch for plinth.

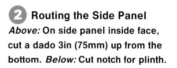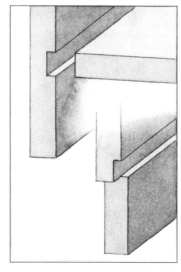

3 **Routing the Central Divider**
Above: Cut a dado 3in (75mm) up from bottom on both faces of divider. *Below:* Cut notch at base for plinth.

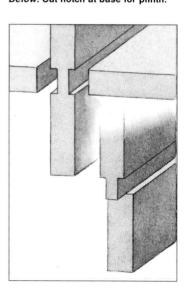

Swing-door Wardrobe

Top Fastening

Stand the top panel on its back edge and offer up to the dado in the left-hand side panel and locate on to the central divider. Glue and screw through the left-hand side panel into the edge of the top panel (fig. 1, below). Drill and countersink the top panel from the outside into the center of the dado in five places and glue and screw through the top into the central divider.

Right-hand Side Assembly

Drill and countersink through the right-hand side panel from the outside through the top and bottom dados for five fastenings in each joint. Put the right-hand base panel in position. Offer up the side panel, trapping the base, and glue and screw into the top and base.

Glue and screw a corner fixing block (cut from a scrap of wood) under the base, screwing into the central divider and up into the base panel, to secure the base panel at the left-hand end (fig. 2, below).

Plinth

Cut the plinth to the full width of the unit and 3in (75mm) high. Drill, countersink, and then glue and screw into the notches in the uprights in two places (fig. 3, above). Also drill, countersink, and screw down through the front of the base panels into the plinth edge. This completes the main section.

Fitting In Position

If fitting the unit to a wall at the end, fix 1 × 1in (25 × 25mm) battens to the full height of the side panels, on the outside, set 2in (50mm) back from the front edge (fig. 3, below). Later, the scribing fillets will be fastened to these battens so that the unit appears to be fitted tightly to the wall, with no unsightly gaps.

Measure the diagonals of the unit, which should be equal, to ensure the unit is square, and hold it square by nailing a temporary bracing batten across the front.

The unit can now be stood upright and screwed in position against the wall using angled fixing

plates in several unobtrusive places to make the unit absolutely secure. Make sure the unit remains perfectly square as you do this.

Pigeon-hole Units

These units are made up separately and then fitted into the main section as complete units.

The units are 12in (300mm) deep and are fitted flush with the back. Measure the internal width of both right- and left-hand sections. The top and bottom pigeon-hole panels will be this length, less $\frac{15}{16}$in (24mm).

Cut out the top and bottom panels. To make the pigeon-holes square, take the internal width of one section, subtract the combined thickness of the dividers and ends (in our case, $2\frac{3}{8}$in [60mm]), and divide by the number of required spaces (in our case, four). Our pigeon-holes have internal openings $11\frac{1}{8}$in (283mm) wide. Make the internal height of the pigeon-holes the same as the internal width.

To work out the height of the pigeon-hole ends, add together two times the internal spacing plus the

combined thickness of the top, bottom, and middle shelves ($1\frac{1}{2}$in [36mm]) to give the final length to cut (in our case, $23\frac{3}{4}$in [602mm]). Cut out the ends to length. Cut the internal dividers to the height of the ends, less $\frac{15}{16}$in (24mm).

Cut $\frac{1}{8} × \frac{1}{2}$in (3 × 12mm) housings on the insides of the end panels (see **Swing-door Wardrobe Assembly, page 65**) and on both sides of the dividers on the center lines.

Cut out the shelves to the width of the internal spacing, but allow an extra $\frac{1}{4}$in (6mm) to fit into the dados ($\frac{1}{8}$in [3mm] either end).

Glue up all the dados. Tap the shelves into the dados of the dividers (fig. 4, above). Use a piece of scrap wood to protect the shelves from the hammer blows.

Mark the three center lines on the top and bottom panels for where the dividers will be positioned, then drill and countersink through the top and bottom panels from the outside faces for three fixtures along each line. Glue and screw through the panels into the ends of the dividers (fig. 4, below).

1 Assembling the Main Section
Left: Drill and countersink through left-hand side panel to assemble worktop, shelf, and base panel. **Right:** Offer the central divider up to the left-hand side assembly. **Below:** Glue and screw top panel to side panel and central divider.

2 Right-hand Assembly
Above: Screw through right-hand side panel into base. **Below:** Fit fixing block to right-hand base and divider.

3 Finishing Off Main Section
Above: Screw plinth into notches cut in the uprights. **Below:** Add battens to outside of side panels.

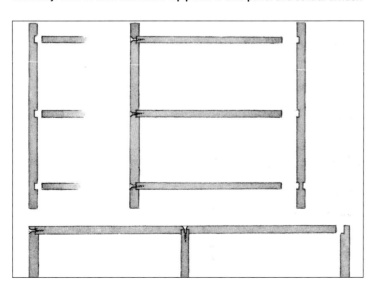

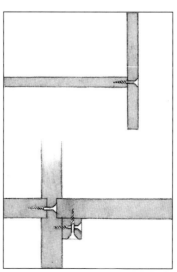

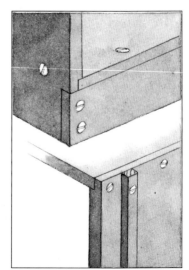

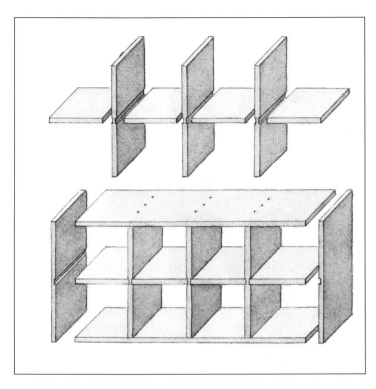

4 Assembling the Pigeon-hole Units

Above: Cut dados across the middles of both sides of the dividers to accept the shelves. *Below:* Cut dados in the top and bottom panels to correspond to positions of dividers; screw in place. Finally add end panels.

5 Fitting the Pigeon-hole Units

Position units flush with back of main section. Screw through from inside into sides and top of wardrobe.

6 Hanging Rail Supports

Use an adjustable bevel to mark off three downward slots as shown at the intervals indicated.

7 Fitting Rail Supports

Screw the supports to the right-hand side of the main section, flush with the front of the pigeon-holes.

Offer up the end panels. Drill and countersink at the top and bottom, and at the middle through the dados, and glue and screw through into the edges of the top, middle, and bottom shelves.

Offer each unit in place and screw through the sides and top from the inside of each pigeon-hole, into the main section (fig. 5). Use four screws in the top of each pigeon-hole and two in the ends of each. Countersink the screws.

HANGING RAIL

Measure from the underside of the pigeon-holes to the base for the length of the hanging rail supports and cut two lengths of 1 × 4in (25 × 100mm) S4S softwood.

Drill a 1in (25mm) diameter hole centrally, with its center 3in (75mm) down from the top (fig. 6), another hole 4in (100mm) below that, and another hole 4in (100mm) below that again. Using an adjustable bevel, mark and cut a 1in (25mm) slot from the top corner down into the top hole. Repeat for parallel slots down to the other holes.

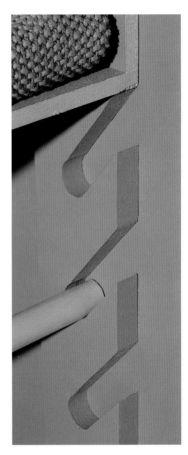

ADJUSTABLE HANGING RAIL

These slots allow you to alter the height of the rail according to the length of clothes hung from it.

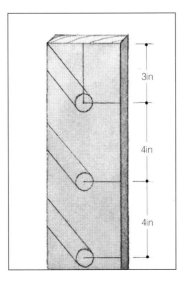

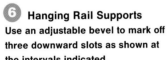

3in

4in

4in

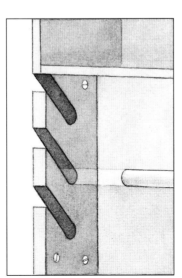

SWING-DOOR WARDROBE

Fit these supports to the side panel and central divider in the right-hand section, with the front edges flush with the fronts of the pigeon-holes (fig. 7, page 71). Fit with pairs of screws down the length. Cut a length of dowel to fit the internal width. This gives an adjustable-height hanging rail.

BASIN

If you are fitting a vanity basin in the worktop in the left-hand unit, fit it at this stage. The basin will be supplied with a template, so place this centrally on the worktop. Either mark around the template onto the worktop, or glue the template in place on the worktop. Use a saber saw to make the cut-out for the basin. Drop it in place and make sure the rim fits snugly against the worktop and that it is level. Remove the basin and apply a bead. of silicone rubber mastic to its lower edge. Replace the basin in the cut-out and secure it to the worktop on the underside using clips supplied by the manufacturer.

Employ a plumber to fit the taps and waste outlet and to make all the necessary connections.

DOWNSTAND

This strengthens the front edge of the worktop. Cut a 1 × 2in (25 × 50mm) batten to the internal width of the left-hand section. Drill and countersink through the worktop into the batten in five places and glue and screw to the underside of the worktop, flush with the front.

DOOR

Calculate the width of the door by measuring from the outside edge of the unit to the nearest edge of the central divider (in our case, a width of 47⅝in [1210mm]).

For the height, measure from the top of the unit to the underside of the base (ie, the top of the plinth) – in our case 69in (approximately 1755mm). Remember to allow for the thickness of any lipping.

Cut out the door and hinge it to the edge of the central divider using four screen hinges (fig. 1).

Fit magnetic catches to the inside of both side panels, and catch plates to both sides of the door.

If you haven't enough space for the swing of the door, cut the door down the middle and hinge the parts together using butt or folding door hinges. The latter are easier to fit because they do not need recessing. You will need to fit a handle near the hinged edge to pull the door open on one side because the hinges will only open one way. Alternatively, fit screen hinges so the door opens in either direction.

TOY BOX

Glue and screw the front, back, and sides together at the corners (see **Toy Box Assembly**). The sides are fitted between front and back panels with five countersunk screws down each edge. Screw 1 × 1in (25 × 25mm) battens to the inside faces of the sides, front, and back, ⅜in (10mm) up from the bottom.

1 **Hinging the Swing-door**
Use four screen hinges to screw inside edge of swing-door to front of central divider.

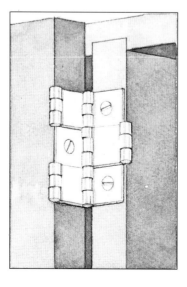

2 **Finger Grip Cut-out**
Above: Make a cut-out in top of toy box front panel. *Below:* Screw lid support batten along inside face.

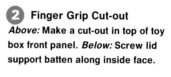
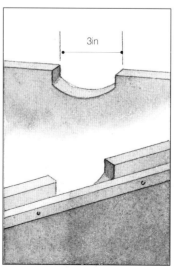

3 **Cut-outs for Lid Pivots**
Above: Box lid pivots on two cut-outs as marked. *Below:* Angle back end of side lid support battens.

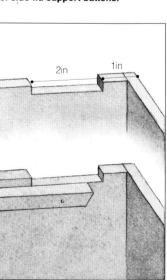

Cut the base to fit the internal dimensions of the box. Drop the base into the box, gluing and nailing it up into the battens.

In the center of the top edge of the front panel, cut out a finger grip hole using a saber saw or a coping saw (fig. 2, above). This should be 3in (75mm) wide and cut down vertically $\frac{11}{32}$in (9mm) curving to a semicircle below this depth.

Make the cut-outs for the lid pivots 2in (50mm) long and $\frac{11}{32}$in (9mm) deep in the top edge of the sides, spaced 1in (25mm) from the back edge (fig. 3).

Fit a 1 × 1in (25 × 25mm) batten to the inside of the front panel (fig. 2, below), $\frac{11}{32}$in (9mm) down from the top edge. Cut battens to fit the sides, running from the front batten to $\frac{5}{16}$in (8mm) short of the back of the pivot cut-outs (fig. 3, below). At the rear end of the batten undercut at an angle of 10 degrees as shown. Fit to the sides by gluing and screwing in three places.

LID

Cut out the lid as specified in the materials list. Place it on top of the box with the back edge just $\frac{1}{16}$in (2mm) inside the inside face of the back panel and mark off the positions of the pivot and finger cut-outs. Cut out the lid to the inside dimensions of the box, leaving the extensions projecting about $\frac{11}{16}$in (17mm) at the pivots (fig. 4), and projecting about 1in (25mm) at the front finger cut-out to act as a handle (see **Toy Box Assembly**).

Fit four castors to the underside of the base for ease of movement.

SCRIBING

Finally, if you are fitting the wardrobe wall-to-wall or in an alcove, finish off using sections of $\frac{5}{32}$in (4mm) plywood scribed to the wall and nailed through into the side panel battens (see **Techniques, page 119**). Paint the scribing fillets to match the color of the wall.

TOY BOX ASSEMBLY

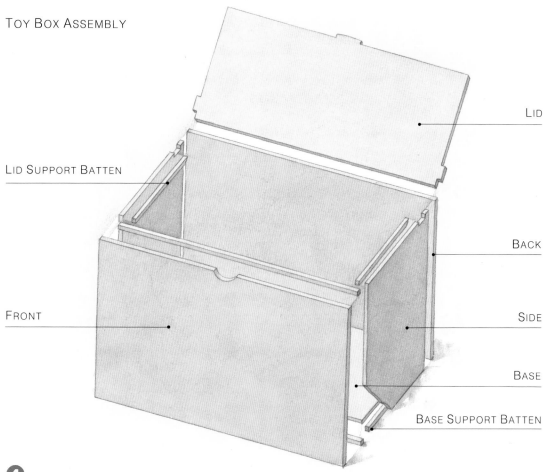

LID

LID SUPPORT BATTEN

BACK

FRONT

SIDE

BASE

BASE SUPPORT BATTEN

4 **Detail of Pivoting Lid**
Lid tongues rest in cut-outs. Angled lid support battens prevent lid slipping when open.

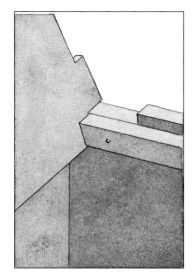

DECORATION

We painted the main section a bold blue, outlining the edges and the frame in yellow. The swing-door offers an opportunity for your imagination to let loose. We stenciled on all of the basic motifs (a quick and easy process) and then decorated these with food labels on the "kitchen" side and wrapping paper on the "shop" side. Simply glue them in place, and apply a coat of varnish when you've finished. Most children would enjoy the chance to help out, cutting up cereal boxes and brightly colored paper, but make sure they are supervised.

ROCKING HORSE

Another nursery classic, the rocking horse satisfies a child's basic desire to make something move. This design, stylized to make it simpler to construct, is nevertheless realistic enough to give the right impression of horsiness.

Traditional rocking horses, which tend to be elaborately carved and finished, are expensive; and the skills required to make such a toy are well beyond most people's abilities. This simple version, with its cheerful finish and lively details – the rope tail and the swiveling ears – would find a welcome home in any child's room.

Although simply painted here, the rocking horse could be decorated in a more ambitious, sophisticated style if your painting skills are sufficiently good. Additionally, the mane could be made from frayed rope so that it matches the tail and a colorful bridle could be tied around the horse's neck.

The body of the horse is composed basically of two sheets of plywood. The two keel-like, half-curved shapes between the plywood body at either end are a safety feature; they prevent the horse being rocked too energetically and toppling over as a result. Like the horse's body, the head, saddle, and ears are cut from a sheet of plywood, which is very economical. Pieces of doweling are used to provide the footrests and handgrips.

ROCKING HORSE

TOOLS

WORKBENCH (fixed or portable)

STEEL MEASURING TAPE

TRY SQUARE

SABER SAW

POWER DRILL

DRILL BIT – $\frac{3}{16}$in (4mm)

COUNTERSINK BIT

SPADE BIT – 1in (25mm) diameter

PANEL SAW

SMOOTHING PLANE (hand or power)

POWER FINISHING SANDER

SCREWDRIVER

ROUTER and ROUNDING-OVER CUTTER

MATERIALS

Part	Quantity	Material	Length
BACKBONE	1	3 × 3in (75 × 75mm) S4S softwood	41in (1040mm)
HEAD	1	$\frac{3}{4}$in (18mm) plywood	Approx. $19\frac{5}{8}$ × $20\frac{7}{8}$in (500 × 530mm)*
SIDE	2	As above	Approx. 17 × 41in (430 × 1040mm)*
BRACING PIECE	2	As above	Approx. 10 × 10in (250 × 250mm)*
SEAT	1	As above	6 × $17\frac{3}{4}$in (150 × 450mm)
EAR	2	As above	Approx. 3 × 5in (75 × 125mm)*
FOOTREST	1	1in (25mm) hardwood doweling	$17\frac{1}{4}$in (440mm)
HANDGRIP	1	As above	9in (230mm)
* Cut from scale pattern provided on page 77			

You can have almost as much fun yourself making this stylized rocking horse as young children will have playing on it. You can follow our grid designs to make up paper patterns or cardboard templates for the head and ears. Alternatively, you can make the head more or less any shape you like, allowing you to stamp your own personality on this comparatively easy-to-make activity toy: there's nothing to restrict you to a rocking horse, and you may prefer to make the head to look like a sheep, a pig, a cat, or a dog.

Most of the parts are made from $\frac{3}{4}$in (18mm) plywood. The semi-circular side pieces that form the "body" are joined at the top by a softwood "backbone" and are braced by gussets at the front and back. The braces ensure that the side pieces form a sturdy "base" on which to rock, and also form stops to prevent the horse from rocking too vigorously and tipping over.

MAKING A START

You will need to make paper patterns or templates for the sides and bracing pieces, and on these you should mark the positions for the footrests and handgrips. Make the patterns from thick brown paper (though newspaper will do if you treat it carefully); cardboard templates are best if more than one rocking horse is to be made. Using a pencil, draw a 4 × 4in (100 × 100mm) grid on the paper and follow the shapes on our grid to produce full-size patterns of a side panel, head, ear, and front brace. Cut out these patterns and temporarily paste or stick them to the plywood for accurate cutting out. On the head, mark the centerpoint of the handle, and on the side pattern mark the centerpoint of the footrest position. Where two pieces of the same shape are required, such as the sides, use the patterns to cut out the first piece, and use this piece as a template to draw around and mark the second piece, which can then be cut out.

BACKBONE

Cut the backbone to length from S4S (smooth 4 sides) softwood. Cut a mortise slot 1in (25mm) from one end right through the lumber (fig. 1). The mortise is for the head to fit into and should be $\frac{3}{4}$in (18mm) wide and 11in (280mm) long.

Bevel the sides of the backbone by about 20 degrees on each side to leave a flat surface centered across the top so that it is about $\frac{13}{16}$in (20mm) wide.

HEAD

Cut the head to shape from the pattern, with the tenon (tongue) at the bottom to fit into the mortise (slot) in the backbone (fig. 1, above). Round over the edges of the head, except for the tenon, either using a router fitted with a rounding-over cutter, or by hand using a spokeshave. Use your full-size pattern to mark the handle position on the head, and with the head held flat on a piece of scrap board, drill through at this point using a 1in (25mm) diameter spade bit.

1 Shaping the Backbone

Above: Finished, beveled backbone has a mortise slot cut 1in (25mm) from one end to accommodate the horse's head. *Below:* Bevel the sides of the backbone by about 20 degrees so that the top face is $\frac{13}{16}$in (20mm) wide.

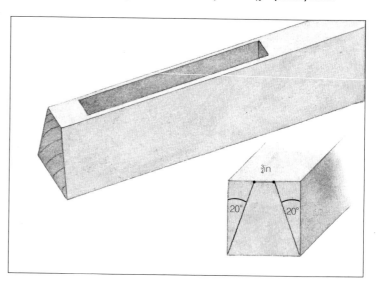

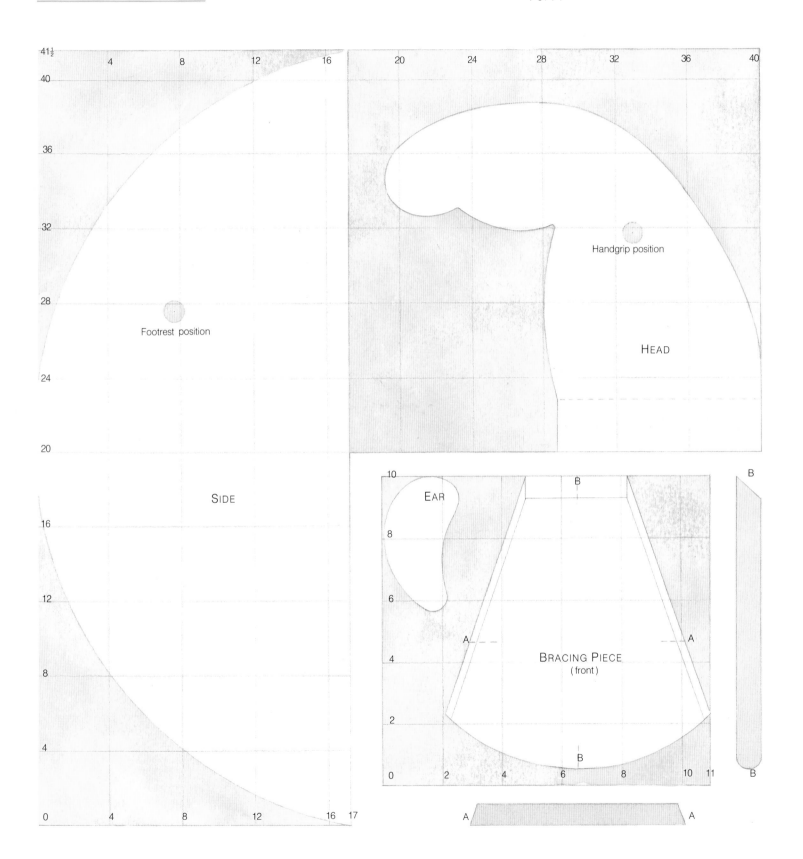

ROCKING HORSE

ROCKING HORSE ASSEMBLY

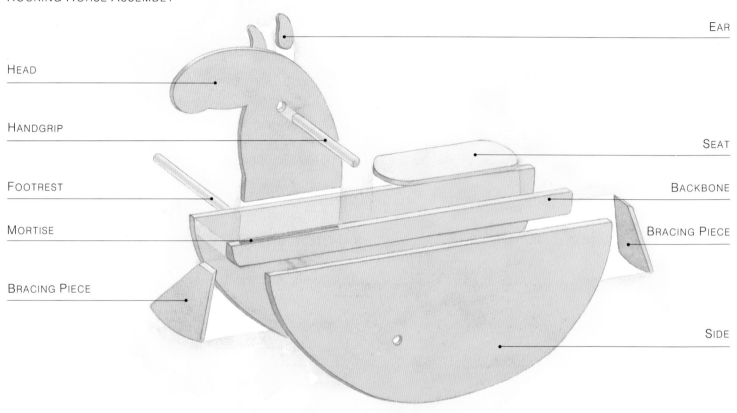

EAR

HEAD

HANDGRIP

SEAT

FOOTREST

BACKBONE

MORTISE

BRACING PIECE

BRACING PIECE

SIDE

1 **Temporary Assembly of the Main Parts**
Above: Temporarily screw head in backbone mortise: turn over and plane off protruding part of tenon. *Below:* Temporarily screw sides to backbone: plane tops of sides level with backbone and curve the ends of the backbone.

2 **Final Front Assembly**
The front of the backbone is curved in line with the side pieces, the edges of which are rounded over.

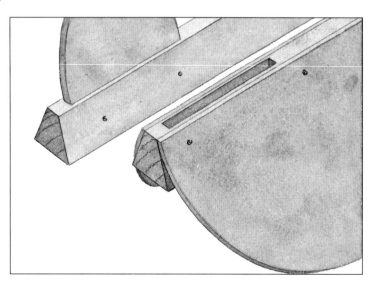

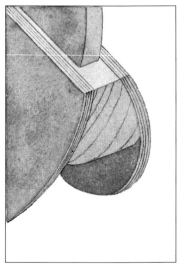

Fit the head into the mortise in the backbone and temporarily screw it in place; then either plane off the protruding part of the tenon flush, or sand it flush using a belt sander. Remove the head.

SIDES

Use the pattern to cut out the two sides. Cut one side to shape, sanding it to a smooth curve if necessary, then use this first side as a template to mark out and cut an identical second side. Using the rounding-over cutter or a spokeshave, round over the curved edges of the sides.

Sand the edges smooth, and, using the pattern, transfer the centerpoints of the footrest positions to the sides. Don't drill these holes yet.

SHAPING THE ENDS OF THE BACKBONE

Temporarily screw the sides to the backbone with four screws along each side and plane the top edges of the sides level with the top of the backbone. Mark off the curve of the sides on to the backbone at both ends (fig. 1, below). Dismantle the sides and cut the backbone to the marked curves. Use a saber saw to trim the ends as close as possible to the lines, then smooth off using a belt sander or power sander.

ASSEMBLY

Glue the head into the mortise in the backbone with aliphatic resin adhesive and then screw it in place with four No. 8 screws. Insert the screws from both sides so that the head is firmly fastened. Glue and screw the sides in place using four countersunk screws on each side.

BRACING PIECES

The bracing pieces serve two purposes: they brace the sides rigid, and they act as stops to restrict over-enthusiastic rocking action.

Use the pattern to mark out the bracing pieces and cut them out. The edges must be beveled as shown on the pattern. This is done either by tilting the saw blade while cutting out, or by planing the edges after the pieces have been cut out. Round over the bottom edges of the braces to give a curved finish.

Slide the braces into place between the sides, and adjust their positions until the curved bottom edges coincide with the curved bottom edges of the horse's sides. Drill pilot holes through the sides of the rocking horse into the edges of the bracing pieces, then glue and screw in place using four No. 8 countersunk screws each side.

SEAT

Cut out the seat panel. Use a paint can to mark half-rounds at each end, then cut these out using a Saber saw. Round over the edges as before. Glue and screw the seat down on to the backbone, about $1\frac{1}{2}$in (40mm) back from the head.

FOOTREST AND HANDGRIP

Drill through the sides horizontally to take the footrest. At the marked positions, drill 1in (25mm) diameter holes horizontally and square to the backbone. It is best to get a helper with a good eye to line up the drill for you. Cut the footrest dowel to length, round over the ends, and slide the dowel into position (fig. 4). Fit it in place with a dab of glue. Cut the handgrip dowel to length, round over the ends, and fit it with glue in the hole drilled through the head.

EARS

Use the pattern to mark out the ears. Cut them out using a saber saw, then round over the edges. Screw the ears in place on either side of the head (fig. 5), offsetting them slightly so that the screw positions do not coincide. Countersink the screws. Do not glue the ears – this allows them to swivel, an amusing touch that also reduces impact danger.

TAIL

Drill a hole the thickness of the tail rope centrally in the end of the backbone to a depth of about 2in (50mm). Use a piece of rope about 18in (450mm) long and glue one end into the hole, then tease out the other end to give a tassle.

Paint the horse as required. The finish here is very basic, but you could paint it more intricately to look like a fairground attraction, time and skill permitting.

❸ Fitting the Bracing Pieces
Bracing pieces front and back are glued and screwed in place through the side panel.

❹ View of the Underside
Note how the two bracing pieces are angled outward and protrude beyond curved sides to act as stops. Footrest dowel feeds through holes drilled in sides, and seat is placed across top of backbone.

❺ Handgrip and Ears
Round over ends of handgrip and glue in place. Screw the ears to sides of head so that they swivel.

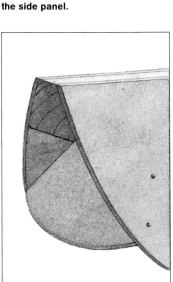

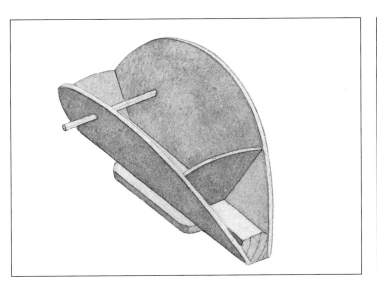

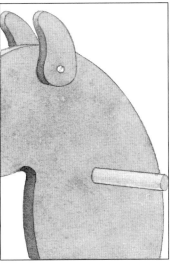

PUPPET THEATER

Giving hours of amusement as the focus of children's theatrical interest and skills, this grand and exciting puppet theater would make a superb Christmas present. It has been designed for use with marionettes, and is tall and deep enough for productions to be easily staged. The theater can be easily dismantled and packed entirely flat when not in use, or it could provide a focal point in a child's bedroom or playroom, or even in the corner of the living room. Although it looks imposing, it takes time rather than money to make, and it is not demanding in terms of woodworking skills.

Based on a traditional design, the theater consists of a front "proscenium" arch whose sides curve around to support a backdrop flat, a middle section with a staircase at one side going up to a balcony, and a rear section comprising two L-shaped portions which frame another flat. Below the balcony, doors open to reveal another view. The entire effect is very theatrical, with a sense of different spaces opening up, false perspectives, and light filtering in from the sides. The three flats can be painted on both sides to provide twice as many scenes, and extra ones can be made later on for new shows.

The theater is constructed from thin plywood and battens. Although construction is very simple and no joining is required, the stairs are rather tricky to make and the middle section would be simpler if you omitted them. The main skill required is the ability to cut out each section accurately so that individual parts slot correctly onto the locating pieces screwed to the base.

Undecorated, the theater has a strong architectural character. For decoration, copy details from cut-out paper theaters or adopt a simpler style if you are not confident about your painting skills.

PUPPET THEATER

Youngsters will keep themselves amused for hours with this traditional puppet theater, making up and performing their own plays.

The theater is made entirely from $\frac{3}{16}$in (4mm) plywood – the cheap interior-quality redwood type is fine – and 1 × 1in (25 × 25mm) S4S (smooth 4 sides) softwood battens to strengthen the frame. The base section which forms the stage is supported by a framework of 1 × 2in (25 × 50mm) S4S softwood.

The theater is made up in four parts – the front section, the central section, the back section, and the base – and has three different flats for changes of scenery which can be painted on both sides for twice as many backdrops. The sides are kept open to allow the puppets to be brought on and off the stage.

TOOLS

WORKBENCH (fixed or portable)

STEEL MEASURING TAPE

TRY SQUARE

POWER SABER SAW

POWER DRILL

DRILL BIT – $\frac{3}{16}$in (4mm)

PAIR OF C-CLAMPS

SMOOTHING PLANE (hand or power)

POWER FINISHING SANDER or HAND SANDING BLOCK

LIGHTWEIGHT HAMMER

COPING SAW – for cutting stairway tread slots

MATERIALS

Part	Quantity	Material	Length
FRONT SECTION			
FRONT ARCH SECTION	2	$\frac{3}{16}$in (4mm) redwood plywood	$31\frac{1}{2} \times 39$in (800 × 1000mm)
SIDE WING	2	As above	$10\frac{3}{4} \times 31\frac{1}{2}$in (270 × 800mm)
FRONT FLAT SUPPORT	4	As above	$6 \times 31\frac{1}{2}$in (150 × 800mm)
FRONT FLAT	1	As above	$29\frac{1}{8} \times 31\frac{1}{2}$in (740 × 800mm)
SPACING BATTEN	2	1 × 1in (25 × 25mm) S4S softwood	$30\frac{3}{4}$in (780mm)
SPACING BATTEN	4	As above	$31\frac{1}{2}$in (800mm)
CURTAIN POLE	1	$\frac{1}{2}$in (12mm) dowel	39in (1000mm)
CENTRAL SECTION			
CENTRAL ARCH SECTION	2	$\frac{3}{16}$in (4mm) redwood plywood	$24 \times 31\frac{1}{2}$in (600 × 800mm)
BALCONY SUPPORT	4	As above	$6\frac{3}{4} \times 15\frac{3}{4}$in (173 × 400mm)
BALCONY	1	As above	$13\frac{3}{4} \times 38\frac{1}{2}$in (350 × 990mm)
CENTRAL FLAT	1	As above	$11\frac{1}{2} \times 31\frac{1}{2}$in (290 × 800mm)
STAIRCASE SIDE	2	As above	$10 \times 15\frac{3}{4}$in (250 × 400mm)
STAIRCASE BACK PANEL	1	As above	$5\frac{3}{4} \times 15\frac{3}{4}$in (145 × 400mm)
STAIR TREAD	12	As above	$1\frac{3}{16} \times 6\frac{1}{8}$in (30 × 155mm)
SPACING BATTEN	4	1 × 1in (25 × 25mm) S4S softwood	$31\frac{1}{2}$in (800mm)
SPACING BATTEN	4	As above	$15\frac{3}{4}$in (400mm)
LOCATING PIECE	2	As above	Approx. $5\frac{5}{8}$in (130mm)
BALCONY STIFFENING PIECE	As required	As above	Cut to fit from approx. $11\frac{1}{2}$ft (3.5m)
BACK SECTION			
BACK FLAT SUPPORT	4	$\frac{3}{16}$in (4mm) redwood plywood	$12 \times 31\frac{1}{2}$in (300 × 800mm)
BACK WING	2	As above	$18\frac{3}{4} \times 31\frac{1}{2}$in (475 × 800mm)
BACK FLAT	1	As above	$17\frac{1}{4} \times 31\frac{1}{2}$in (440 × 800mm)
SPACING BATTEN	4	1 × 1in (25 × 25mm) S4S softwood	$31\frac{1}{2}$in (800mm)
BASE SECTION			
STAGE	1	$\frac{3}{16}$in (4mm) redwood plywood	41 × 41in (1040 × 1040mm)
STAGE PLINTH	2	1 × 2in (25 × 50mm) S4S softwood	41in (1040mm)
STAGE PLINTH	7	As above	Cut to fit
LOCATING PIECE	19	1 × 1in (25 × 25mm) S4S softwood	Cut to fit

Also required: canvas and fabric adhesive for hinges, approx. 5ft (1.5m) of fabric for curtains

PUPPET THEATER ASSEMBLY

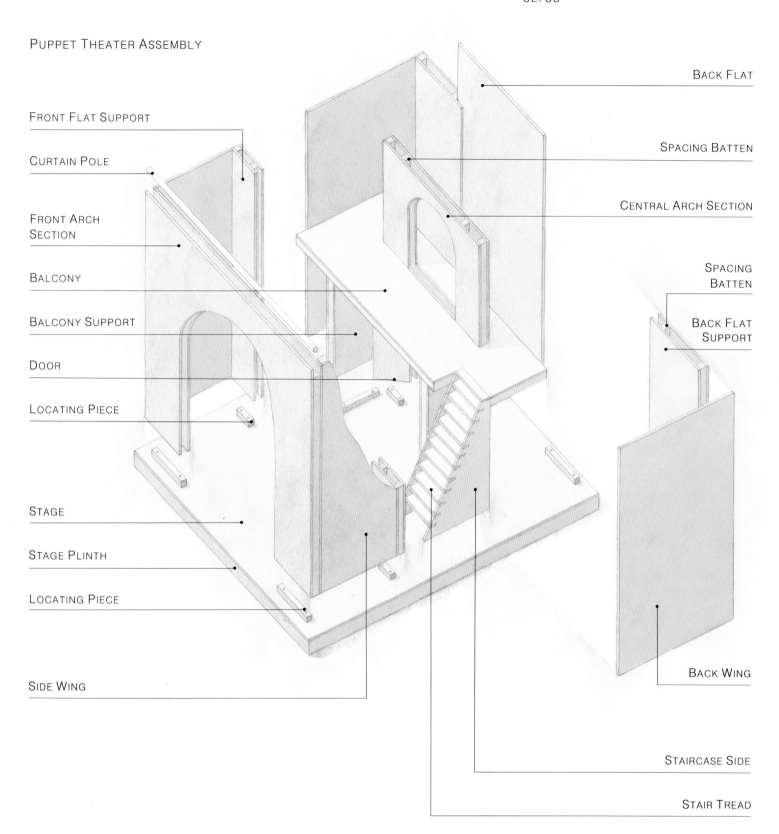

FRONT FLAT SUPPORT

CURTAIN POLE

FRONT ARCH SECTION

BALCONY

BALCONY SUPPORT

DOOR

LOCATING PIECE

STAGE

STAGE PLINTH

LOCATING PIECE

SIDE WING

BACK FLAT

SPACING BATTEN

CENTRAL ARCH SECTION

SPACING BATTEN

BACK FLAT SUPPORT

BACK WING

STAIRCASE SIDE

STAIR TREAD

PUPPET THEATER

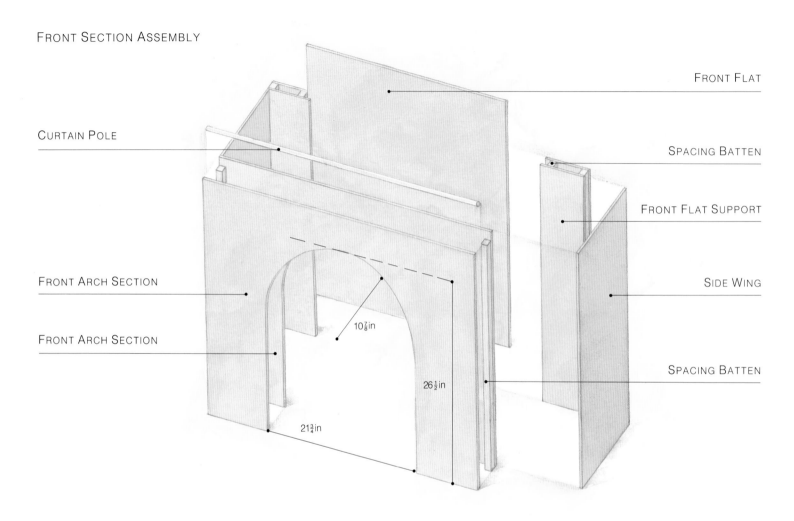

CURTAIN POLE

FRONT ARCH SECTION

FRONT ARCH SECTION

FRONT FLAT

SPACING BATTEN

FRONT FLAT SUPPORT

SIDE WING

SPACING BATTEN

$10\frac{7}{8}$in

$26\frac{1}{2}$in

$21\frac{3}{4}$in

FRONT SECTION

Cut out all of the plywood pieces required for the front section.

On one of the plywood panels for the front arch section, mark out the arch centrally so that it is $21\frac{3}{4}$in (550mm) wide and $26\frac{1}{2}$in (675mm) high, leaving 5in (125mm) of plywood above the top of the curve. Mark out the curve so that it has a radius of $10\frac{7}{8}$in (275mm).

Cut out the arch using a saber saw. Transfer the outline to the other front panel and cut it out; alternatively, clamp the two panels together and cut both pieces simultaneously.

Cut two spacing battens $30\frac{3}{4}$in (780mm) long. Glue and nail them between the two arch panels, flush with the side and bottom edges (*see* **Front Section Assembly**). This leaves space for the curtain pole to sit on top of the battens and the curtains to be drawn back.

Cut four spacing battens $31\frac{1}{2}$in (800mm) long, and glue and nail two between each pair of front flat support panels. One batten is flush with the edges of the plywood, the other is $\frac{3}{4}$in (about 20mm) in from the opposite edges to allow the front flat to slot in place (fig. 1). The flat can be painted both sides to allow different scene changes.

SIDE WINGS

The two side wings are attached to the front arch section and the two front flat supports with long canvas hinges (fig. 2). This allows the side wings and front flat supports to be folded flat against the front arch section for packing away. Cut four strips of canvas $31\frac{1}{2}$in (800mm) long. Using fabric adhesive, glue two of these to the insides of the front arch section and the side wings so that the sides are flush with the edges of the front section. Glue the other two strips to the outside of the side wings at the back to join them to the front flat supports.

CURTAIN POLE

The curtain pole is a 39in (1000mm) long piece of doweling that rests on top of the spacing battens in the front section (*see* **Front Section Assembly**). Once the curtains have been made and threaded onto it, the dowel can be nailed in place down into the batten at both ends.

CENTRAL SECTION

Cut out all the plywood pieces for the central arch section, including the central flat, the balcony, and the balcony supports.

On the central arch section, two cut-outs are required for doorways (fig. 3). On one of the arch section plywood panels, mark out the lower doorway and top arch centrally, 10in (250mm) wide. Mark the lower doorway 12in (300mm) high. For the top arch, mark the base line 16in (405mm) up from the bottom and 14in (355mm) high. The radius of the top curve is 5in (125mm), leaving 1½in (about 40mm) of plywood above the arch (fig. 3).

Cut out the doorway and arch using a saber saw, then use the cut-out panel as a template to transfer the marks to the other panel; alternatively, clamp the panels together and cut out both pieces simultaneously. Keep one of the lower door cut-outs to make into a pair of doors for the lower doorway later on.

From 1 × 1in (25 × 25mm) S4S softwood, cut four lengths of spacing batten, each 31½in (800mm) long. Glue and nail these between the two plywood arch panels, one down each long edge, and one ¾in (about 20mm) in from each edge of the doorway cut-outs (fig. 3).

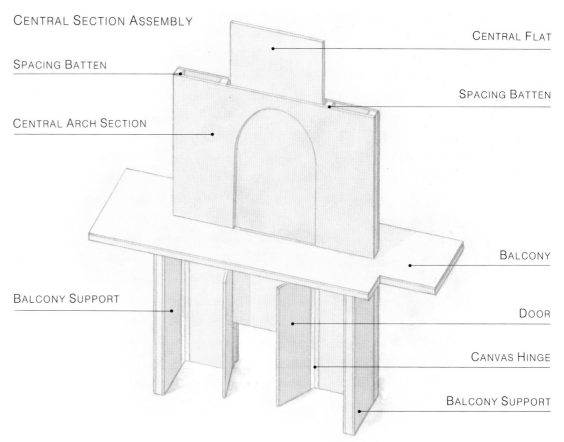

CENTRAL SECTION ASSEMBLY

CENTRAL FLAT

SPACING BATTEN

SPACING BATTEN

CENTRAL ARCH SECTION

BALCONY

BALCONY SUPPORT

DOOR

CANVAS HINGE

BALCONY SUPPORT

❶ Front Flat Supports
Position spacing battens; one flush with panel edges, the other inset ¾in (20mm) from opposite edges.

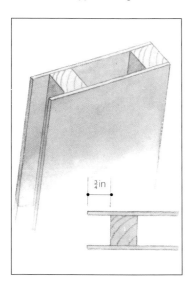

❷ Hinging the Front Section
Above left: **Fabric-hinge inside of side wings to back of front arch section.**
Above right: **Fabric-hinge outside face of side wings to outside edges of front flat supports.** *Below:* **Plan view shows how front section folds flat for storage.**

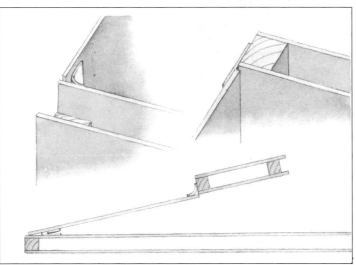

❸ Central Arch Section
Make cut-outs for two doorways; cut both central arch panels and join using four spacing battens.

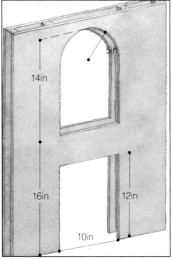

PUPPET THEATER

BALCONY SUPPORTS

Cut four spacing battens, $15\frac{3}{4}$in (400mm) long. Glue and nail these between the balcony support pieces, flush with both edges (fig. 1).

Make hinges for the supports by cutting two lengths of canvas, $15\frac{3}{4}$in (400mm) long. Fabric-hinge the supports to the front of the bottom half of the central section so that each support is flush with an outside edge (fig. 1).

DOUBLE DOORS

Saw one of the lower door cut-outs in two lengthwise to make a pair of doors. Make hinges for the doors by cutting two lengths of canvas 12in (300mm) long. Fabric-hinge the doors to the front of the central section on either side of the lower opening (fig. 2).

BALCONY

The balcony needs a cut-out on the front right-hand corner to take the staircase. This cut-out should be $6\frac{1}{8}$in (155mm) wide and 4in (100mm) deep (fig. 3, above).

1 Balcony Supports
The balcony support pieces are fabric-hinged to central arch section flush with outside edges.

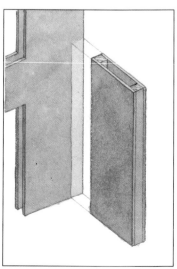

The central arch section fits into a slot cut into the balcony. This slot measures $24\frac{1}{8}$in (602mm) long and $1\frac{3}{16}$in (30mm) wide, and is situated centrally on the length of the balcony panel and $7\frac{1}{2}$in (193mm) back from the front edge (fig. 3, above). It is important that the slot is precisely positioned, so double check your markings before cutting out. Cut out the slot using a saber saw after first drilling a couple of holes for the blade to go through.

Turn the balcony upside down. Cut lengths of 1×1in (25×25mm) S4S softwood to go all the way around the edges of the balcony on the underside and across it, then glue and nail these in place (fig. 3, below). These balcony stiffening pieces strengthen the floor.

Cut two locating pieces from the 1×1in (25×25mm) S4S softwood, about $5\frac{1}{8}$in (130mm) long; these will fit into the cavities at the top of the two balcony supports (fig. 1). To position these pieces, slot the balcony over the central arch section, turn the assembly upside down, and draw around the balcony supports to mark their positions on the underside of the balcony. Remove the balcony and position the locating pieces centrally in the marked positions. Glue and nail them in place.

CENTRAL FLAT

Cut an $11\frac{1}{2} \times 31\frac{1}{2}$in ($290 \times 800$mm) plywood flat to fit into the central arch section. This can be painted to depict views through the doorway and arch – again, paint both sides of the flat to give a different change of scenery on each side.

STAIRCASE

Cut out the back panel, the two sides and 12 stair treads following the dimensions given in the Materials chart (page 82). The height of the staircase should be to the balcony level, allowing for a $\frac{3}{16}$in (4mm) thick tread which sits on the top of the staircase sides.

Clamp the staircase side pieces together and cut them diagonally through their length so that they are 1in (25mm) wide at the top and 10in (250mm) wide at the bottom.

Mark out 11 equally spaced slots for the treads along the diagonal edge. These should be parallel with the base of the side section and should measure $1\frac{3}{16}$in (30mm) long and $\frac{3}{16}$in (4mm) wide to take the stair treads. The top tread simply sits on top of the staircase (fig. 4).

To make it easier to cut out the slots, drill a $\frac{3}{16}$in (4mm) diameter hole at the end of each slot, then cut down each side of the slot using a back saw if working by hand, or using a power saber saw. To cut exactly matching slots, which is important if the stair treads are to be level, clamp both side panels together and cut out the slots at the same time.

Glue and nail the back panel in place between the two sides, flush at the back. Glue and nail the top tread in place, then glue and slide in the bottom one, using aliphatic resin adhesive. Allow the adhesive to set, then glue and slot in all the other treads, keeping a tight fit for maximum strength. When dry, sand down the ends of the stair treads flush with the side panels.

BACK SECTION

Cut out from the plywood the back flat, the four back flat support panels, and the two back wings following the Materials chart (page 82).

Cut four lengths of spacing batten $31\frac{1}{2}$in (800mm) long and make up the two back flat supports in the same way as the front flat supports, with the battens sandwiched between the panels. Two battens should be glued and nailed flush with the outer edges of the panels, and the other two should be set $\frac{3}{4}$in (about 20mm) in from the inner edges to form a slot into which the back flat will slide.

Fabric-hinge the two back wings onto the back flat supports (fig. 1, page 88) so that they can be folded either way to allow use of both sides for scene changes, and to allow the section to fold flat for storage.

Cut the back flat $31\frac{1}{2}$in (800mm) high and $17\frac{1}{4}$in (440mm) wide to fit between the flat supports. Again, this flat can be painted on both sides with different scenes.

2 Adding the Doors
Make a pair of doors from one of the lower cut-outs; fabric-hinge them to the central arch section.

3 Making the Balcony
Above: Measure accurately for cut-outs in middle to take central arch section and in right-hand corner for staircase. *Below:* Add battens to underside of balcony for strength, plus two locating pieces to fit in balcony supports.

4 Making the Staircase
Glue and nail the back between the sides. The top stair tread sits on top, the others slot in place.

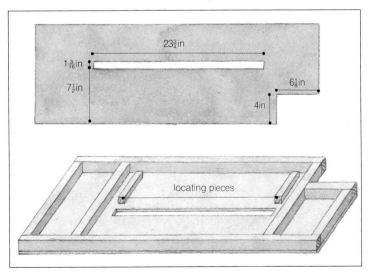

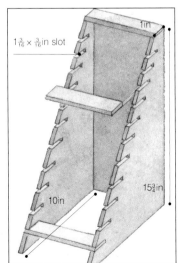

PUPPET THEATER

BASE SECTION

Cut out this section to form a stage 41in (1040mm) square. This will be large enough to allow about ¾in (20mm) all around the theater when all the pieces are in place.

For the stage plinth, we used 1 × 2in (25 × 50mm) S4S softwood. This is nailed to the underside of the stage, flush with the edges all the way around and across the middle to act as strengthening (fig. 2). Cut two battens to the full length of the stage to fit flush along the front and back edges. Cut three more battens to fit exactly between these first two lengths – two to fit flush along the sides, and the third to sit midway between them. Finally, cut four lengths of batten to fit flush between the battens at the sides and the batten halfway across.

Glue and nail up the strengthening framework of battens, then glue and nail the stage panel on top, securing through the plywood into the lumber framework.

Sand all of the edges flush.

LOCATING PIECES

These lengths of 1 × 1in (25 × 25mm) batten are positioned on the base section to hold the front, central, and back sections in place (see **Puppet Theater Assembly, page 83**). Cut the battens to lengths that will allow them to fit *loosely* inside all of the box sections that will be standing on the base.

To position the locating pieces, stand the three sections in place on the base with roughly ¾in (20mm) lip all around. Make sure that the stage plinths that run to the full length are positioned at the front and the back, since the front plinth will be visible to the audience. Either mark around the box section onto the base using a pencil, or measure in for their positions. Remove the sections, and mark the positions for the locating pieces, allowing for the width of the plywood of the box sections and for the spacing battens. Then glue and screw the locating pieces in place, and check that they are correctly positioned by repositioning the front, back, and central sections.

FINISHING

For a really splendid, theatrical look, it is worth spending that extra bit of time making sure that you get the details just right.

CURTAINS

For curtains that pull across, allow one and a half to twice the width of the arch, divided into two to make two curtains. The width for the curtains depends on how thick the fabric is, as you will probably want the curtains to pull back completely into the sides of the arch section. Allow extra fabric on the sides for turning and neatening the edges, and about 3in (75mm) on the length to allow for a hem at the bottom and turning over at the top to take the curtain pole (fig. 3).

Cut out the fabric and hand- or machine-stitch the sides and hem. Turn over the top edge to make a casing, and thread the curtain pole through. Place the pole across the front arch section and nail it down on to the battens at both ends.

For decorative effect, you could tie the curtains back, leaving them in full view as shown in the photographs (opposite). We also glued a remnant of fabric at the top of the arch for a pelmet or valence.

PAINT EFFECTS

We painted the flat supports and wings of the theater in bold, contrasting colors. The front of the theater, however, shows just how spectacular the finished effect can be. The paint is applied in quite an impressionistic fashion, and the details then inked in with a black marker pen. This is undeniably ambitious, and you may not think your own skills can match those shown here. You can still attempt a fair imitation, however: the design consists of a series of boxes and panels, and it would be relatively straightforward to paint these in over a background color, and then to add a few details.

On the flats, a field of grass, a beach, or a sky at night can all be depicted with as much or as little detail as you choose.

---

1 Hinging the Back Section
Above: Fabric-hinge back wings to back flat supports on the outside.
Below: Plan shows back folded flat.

2 Making the Base Section
Glue and nail 1 × 2in (25 × 50mm) strengthening battens around the perimeter of the underside of the stage, another across the middle, and four more to fit between the side and middle battens.

3 Adding the Curtains
Turn over the top edge of the curtains to make a casing through which to thread the curtain pole.

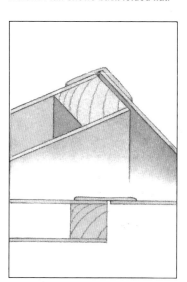

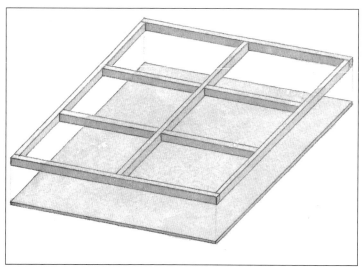

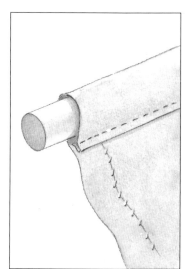

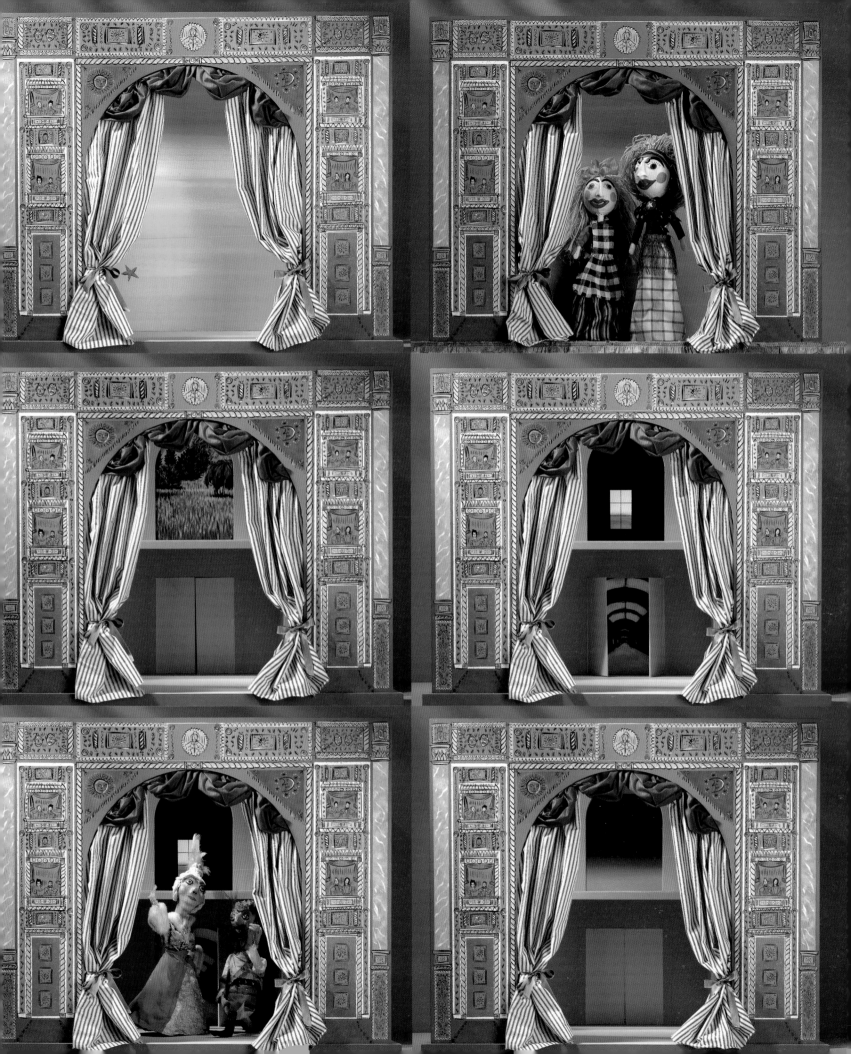

BLACKBOARD SCREEN

This blackboard screen is just the job for encouraging self-expression. Presented with the screen and a handful of colored chalks, no child will be able to resist drawing or writing on it. It is an entertainment and educational aid rolled into one.

The beauty about making your own board instead of simply buying one is that it can be far, far bigger and so much more appealing to young eyes. By linking three boards together, you can create a screen with half a dozen surfaces which can be used to hide clutter quickly at the end of playtime.

A maximum safe height for the screen is about 48in (1220mm). Anything much taller encourages smaller children to climb onto furniture in order to reach the top.

Also, a height of 48in (1220mm) is convenient and economical as it can be cut from a 48in (1220mm) square sheet of medium-density fiberboard (MDF). Three screens can be cut from the width, each being 16in (400mm) wide. Of course, you can make any size screen you prefer.

The hinges you choose will dictate the thickness of board to buy, so buy the hinges first, checking with the manufacturer's advice, then buy the boards. Use three hinges between each pair of screens. Cabinet hinges are usually used with a minimum board thickness of $\frac{5}{8}$in (15mm). These are face-fitted so you don't have to cut hinge slots. Screen hinges enable the screens to fold in any direction for flexibility (fig. 1). They are usually used with boards 1in (25mm) thick.

Paint the boards with two coats of blackboard paint before you fit the hinges. It is quick-drying so the coats can be applied soon after each other – check the manufacturer's instructions for precise times, but allow 24 hours after the second coat before use. Blackboard paint is available in fairly small quantities so there will be little waste.

SCREEN TEST

Painted in bold colors on the other side, the screen will instantly hide a messy corner.

The screen is free-standing but a base can be added. This is important if children are going to use the blackboard element, since the pressure they exert when chalking may tip the screen over.

A simple base can be made by screwing a pair of 2in (50mm) square battens to a 1in (25mm) thick base of chipboard or MDF for each board of the screen. The gap between the battens should be very slightly greater than the thickness of the boards so they slot comfortably into place but are held firmly (fig. 2). The detachable bases allow the boards of the screen to be folded flat when not in use.

1 Fitting the Hinges

Screen hinges screwed to the edges of adjacent boards enable screen to be folded in either direction.

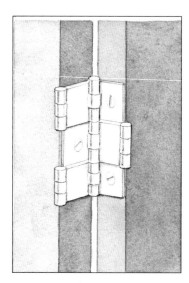

2 Detachable Base

Screw a pair of 2 × 2in (50 × 50mm) battens to a piece of board so that screen will slot firmly in place.

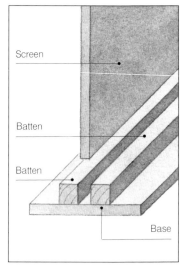

Screen

Batten

Batten

Base

TRUCK DESK

The neat thing about this attractive truck desk is the small amount of wall space it takes up, and the compact "box" it forms when shut in which to tuck away homework and reference books when not in use. The wing mirrors also let you see who's coming up behind!

The basic desk unit is made from $\frac{1}{2}$in (12mm) medium-density fiberboard (MDF) or plywood, with $\frac{3}{4}$in (18mm) thick MDF or plywood used for the drop-down writing flap, and $1\frac{1}{2} \times 6$in (38×150mm) smooth 4 sides (S4S) lumber for the tires and back of the cab. The whole unit is 49$\frac{1}{4}$in (1250mm) high and 35$\frac{1}{2}$in (900mm) wide. When closed it protrudes 10$\frac{1}{2}$in (268mm) from the wall; with the writing flap down it protrudes 24$\frac{1}{4}$in (618mm).

The writing flap measures 15$\frac{3}{4} \times 35\frac{1}{2}$in (400 × 900mm); it is the same width and height as the desk unit which is 7in (180mm) deep. It is open-topped, with a shelf 4in (100mm) beneath the top edge.

The tires and cab sections are screwed to the wall first. They are cut to a length of 49$\frac{1}{4}$in (1250mm) and

shaped at the top to form the driver's cab (fig. 1). The top of the cab is a 1$\frac{1}{2}$in (38mm) wide strip of lumber cut from a 19$\frac{3}{4}$in (500mm) length of 1$\frac{1}{2} \times 6$in (38×150mm) timber. The rest of this piece, approximately 4$\frac{1}{4}$in (110mm) wide, forms the lower edge of the cab rear window.

The desk section is made up as shown (fig. 2). The desk unit is screwed to the cab uprights so it just covers the bottom of the cab rear window. The writing flap is grooved on its front face to look like planks, and has two $\frac{1}{2} \times 3 \times 15\frac{3}{4}$in (12 × 75 × 400mm) battens fitted to it to represent a tail gate. It is hinged to the lower edge of the desk unit and is secured with two short chains so that it opens level.

The final embellishments to add (all from $\frac{1}{2}$in [12mm] MDF) are a chassis piece fitted to the wall under the desk unit; an axle fitted 12in (300mm) up from the floor; a 5in (130mm) diameter disc planted on the axle to represent the differential case; two mudguards; rear lights; and wing mirrors. Lastly, glue a cut-out of the driver in the cab.

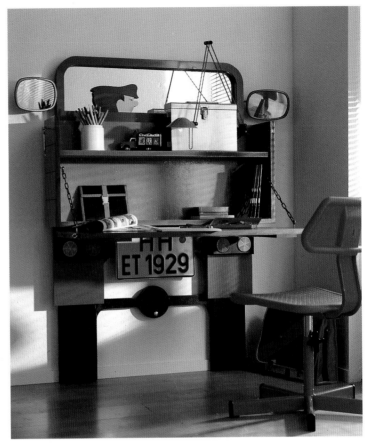

① Forming the Back Cut-outs
Cut the tire and cab sections from 1$\frac{1}{2} \times 6$in (38×150mm) to dimensions shown and screw to wall.

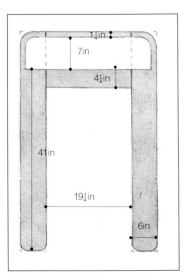

② Forming the Box Section
Use $\frac{1}{2}$in (12mm) board to make a box; fit the top 4in (100mm) down from the top edge of the back section.

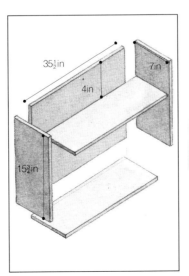

③ Adding the Flap-down Desk
Score the front face to resemble planks and add a "tail gate"; hinge at bottom and secure with chains.

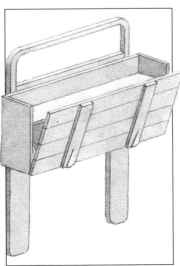

WORKING WONDERS
Homework might get done less reluctantly if a space is set aside and decorated with a witty touch.

PART 3

OUTDOORS

However much space you have, no house is big enough to contain all of a child's prodigious energies. Children need to play outdoors as well as in; they need that sense of physical freedom, distance, and space. In outdoor play children find ways of testing their strengths and skills to the limit; in sports and team games they learn coordination and cooperation.

But a yard is more than just a place where children can kick a ball around. This relatively protected environment provides the child's first contact with nature and growing plants. Here children can learn other skills, such as how to plan a flowerbed, grow vegetables, or take care of animals, and they can take their first steps in understanding the world around them.

Each changing season can bring fresh excitement and entertainment for a child playing outdoors. From building snowmen in winter and watching saplings grow in spring, through playing in a wading pool in summer to catching falling leaves in autumn – the distractions that play outdoors can offer are endless. And apart from being healthy, lots of fresh air tends to tire children out, which is an added bonus for parents!

Outdoors

Play Structures

Ingenuity and imagination are just as important in the design of outdoor play facilities. A simple arrangement of stout rope ladders and swings offers the opportunity for children to try out their skills and test their strength, yet does not look glaringly out of place in the backyard (above). This superb log-cabin play house – half open and half enclosed – has great potential for exploring and make-believe (above right). The witty amusement-park theme of this animal play house, with wild cat slide and giraffe and deer buttresses, makes it irresistible to children (opposite above left). Thick slices of tree trunk are stacked up to make a castle, linked with tree-trunk steps to a drawbridge over a garden stream (opposite above right).

Safety is a key consideration in planning outdoor play areas. Each year, many thousands of children are hurt in accidents that take place on play equipment in their own yards. It must be every parent's responsibility to ensure that such equipment is sturdy and securely anchored, that surfaces are as safe and impact-absorbent as possible, and that children are well supervised, particularly when playing near water or on structures where they can climb high off the ground.

At the same time, an obsession with safety can be counterproductive. Children who are overprotected, without the chance to explore the boundaries of their abilities, are especially vulnerable and through ignorance may take risks in situations where a more experienced child would be wary. Through outdoor play children are able to develop levels of confidence and skill which enable them to meet new experiences safely.

Outdoor Play

With a little planning and some basic training, adults and children can enjoy the outdoors together. As is the case indoors, making positive, well-defined play areas will help to prevent children from taking over completely and overrunning those parts of the yard where adults want to sit and relax. Most yards have potential play areas: an overgrown corner or a neglected patch can provide the perfect spot for children to build a fort or hide out in a secret den. To one side of a terrace, under a pergola or awning, is a good position for a sandbox or sandpit; in poor weather children can still play outside if there is a partially covered area adjacent to the house. Pitches for games should be set out away from flowerbeds full of cherished horticultural specimens and far enough from the house to minimize the risk of a stray ball smashing a window.

In the same way, children will learn to appreciate your gardening efforts if they have a plot of their own. A vegetable patch, a flowerbed, or even a large container full of spring bulbs will provide the means of introducing them to the pleasures of growing plants. Choose relatively quick-growing species for them to tend, so they don't get too impatient waiting for the results: raising sunflowers, zucchini, peas, and carrots gives children immense pleasure. The garden is also the ideal place for observing local wildlife. A shallow pond, visited by frogs and teeming with goldfish, will give hours of rewarding nature study. Putting up bird-tables and nesting boxes will encourage birds to visit your garden.

Children don't need huge, complicated structures to enjoy being outside, but play equipment does help them to explore and to release pent-up energies. Swings, slides, and climbing frames

should be set on a level grassy area or on bark chippings for soft landings, and well within view of the house so you can always keep an eye on things. It is also a good idea, space permitting, to have a paved area where children can ride bikes and skate or pull carts.

Sand and water provide young children with hours of amusement. Sandpits should be covered with a lid when not in use to keep animals from fouling them. Wading pools, old buckets, or plastic bowls full of water are great for splashy, messy games.

Children love to play in small, enclosed spaces. On ground level, you can pitch a tent, improvise a play house from a packing crate (making sure, first, that there are no rough edges) or build a play house from wood for a more permanent attraction. And a tree-house is one of the most magical of all childhood retreats; its appeal will last undimmed for years.

CLIMBING FRAME

Slide, swing, climbing frame, sandpit, and make-believe house – this play structure will be the focus of hours of fun outside. A particular advantage of this structure is its adaptability. You can tailor the size of the frame to suit the amount of space at your disposal; you can vary the width or spacing of the bars; or go on to create a grid-like warren of interconnecting structures following the same basic theme. There is one proviso: the poles should not be required to span a greater distance than about 5ft (1.5m), otherwise they might crack.

Construction depends on a simple system of upright posts and poles. The poles are slotted through holes drilled in the posts and secured by screws at the side; probably the most difficult part of the making is ensuring that the holes are drilled accurately. The sandbox consists of overlapping boards at the sides; the "roof," made of sheets of exterior-grade plywood, has the double purpose of helping to keep the sand dry in rainy weather and giving a suggestion of a play house. The slide platform and slide are also simple to make.

A key safety consideration is ensuring that the entire structure is anchored securely to the ground. There are various ways of achieving this, but one of the most straightforward is to use a post-hole borer to remove the earth and then to concrete the posts firmly in place. Round over the concrete to encourage rainwater to drain away from the posts. And because the frame will be left outdoors in all weather, it is important to buy pressure-treated wood (treated pine is ideal) and to coat it thoroughly with preservative to prolong its life.

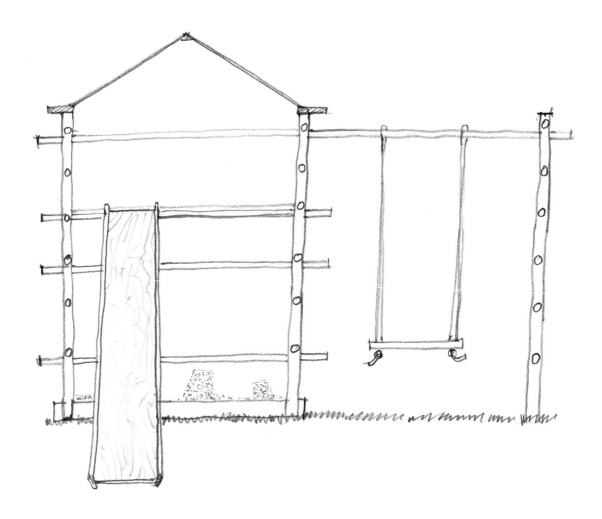

CLIMBING FRAME ASSEMBLY

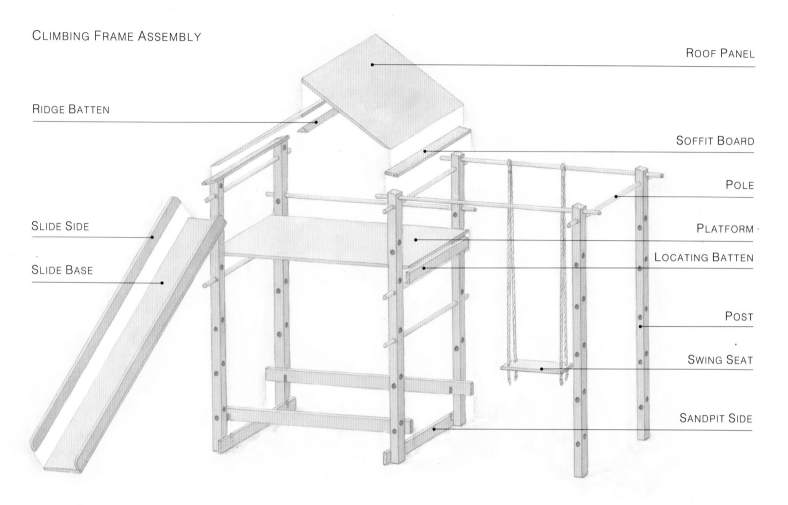

RIDGE BATTEN

SLIDE SIDE

SLIDE BASE

ROOF PANEL

SOFFIT BOARD

POLE

PLATFORM

LOCATING BATTEN

POST

SWING SEAT

SANDPIT SIDE

The design of this climbing frame includes something for children aged between roughly two and seven, so that more than one child in a family can play on it at the same time. For the very young there is a sandpit; the slide will keep older children occupied; and the "house" created by the roof and platform above the sandpit will provide the perfect backdrop for hours of imaginative outdoor play.

The climbing frame *must* be made from pressure-treated lumber and is finished with three or four coats of good-quality, exterior-grade clear varnish. The unpainted finish allows the structure to blend

sympathetically with the garden. Before starting work, steep the ends of the posts that will be below ground in good-quality wood preservative for 24 hours.

This climbing frame is intended for use solely outdoors, since it must be concreted into the ground for stability. It should be sited on a flat area of lawn free of obstacles or hazards; if the lawn is liable to dry out and become very hard in the summer, you should dig a pit around the bottom of the slide and fill it with wood chips or another impact-absorbent material sold specifically for use in playgrounds to reduce the risk of injury.

The framework consists of six posts with holes drilled at intervals down their length through which horizontal poles, $1\frac{1}{4}$in (35mm) in diameter, are slotted to form bars. The number of poles used is optional and their arrangement can be varied quickly and easily since each pole is held in place to the posts with "locking" screws. These screws can be taken out at any time to release a pole. When poles are repositioned, it is essential always to replace the screws and tighten them. It is not necessary to use poles in every hole – gaps can be left according to the sizes and needs of the children using the frame.

The play platform, constructed from solid $\frac{3}{4}$in (18mm) plywood, is secured to its platform with locating battens and turnbuckles.

The removable slide is located on to a supporting pole with two turnbuckles. It can then be taken down and stored when not required for long periods of time.

The swing should be suspended from the highest pole, with poles at the front and back of the swing omitted to allow unhindered movement. The height of the seat above the ground is determined by the age of the children for which it is intended and, subsequently, by the lengths of rope used.

CLIMBING FRAME

TOOLS

TRY SQUARE

STEEL RULE

ADJUSTABLE BEVEL

POWER DRILL and drill bits

SPADE BIT or EXPANSIVE BIT

COUNTERSINK BIT

DRILL STAND

POWER PLANE

POST-HOLE BORER or
NARROW SPADE

CARPENTER'S LEVEL

SMOOTHING PLANE (hand or
power)

POWER ROUTER and
ROUNDING-OVER BIT

POWER FINISHING SANDER or
HAND SANDING BLOCK

CONSTRUCTION

The construction of the frame is straightforward, the most arduous part being the digging of the holes for the six supporting posts. This can be done using a narrow spade, but a post-hole borer – a large, cork-screw-like tool obtainable from a rental shop – makes the task much easier. It is twisted back and forth to make the hole and lifted out to deposit the waste earth.

CUTTING THE POSTS TO LENGTH

Cut the six posts to length: 7ft 6in–8ft (2.45–2.6m) long, according to how high you intend the frame to be above ground. Remember that at least 30in (750mm) of each post should be sunk into the ground and concreted in place.

MARKING THE POSTS

Using a try square, draw a line on all four faces of each post, 30in (750mm) up from the bottom, to mark the earth-level once the posts

are erected. On one face of the post, mark hole positions at 12in (300mm) intervals above the earth-level mark (fig. 1). Make sure that each mark is centrally positioned.

On an adjacent face, mark the first hole 9½in (240mm) up from the earth-level mark. Then work up the post, marking off hole positions at 12in (300mm) intervals as before. This will ensure that the climbing bars are staggered on adjacent sides of the climbing frame (fig. 2).

Mark the five remaining posts in the same way.

MAKING THE HOLES

Drill the holes through the posts using a 1⅜in (36mm) drill or an expansive bit. To ensure that each hole is at the center of the post and is square to the verticals, use a drill stand or use a try square as a visual guide when drilling.

The holes for the locking screws are made in the faces of the posts adjacent to the pole holes. Each screw hole must align with the center of each pole hole. Drill a countersunk clearance hole for a

1½in (37mm) No. 10 woodscrew until the clearance hole meets the larger pole hole. Make sure all the locking screw holes are on what will be the inside faces of the posts.

ASSEMBLING THE FRAME

Cut 21 poles, 1¼in (35mm) in diameter and 59⅝in (1510mm) long; bevel or round over the ends.

Assemble the posts and poles on site. At this stage, insert poles through the holes in the posts evenly all around the frame, even if you intend to omit or redistribute some later. Ensure that the locking screw holes are on the inside faces of the posts and position the poles so that they protrude by 3in (75mm) at each end of the posts.

With all the posts in position, insert the locking screws, driving each one halfway through the poles to make the assembly rigid.

Mark out the six post positions accurately on the ground. Remove the frame and dig post holes about 4in (100mm) in diameter, using either a narrow spade or a post-hole borer. The holes should be 6in

1 Drilling the Posts
Mark ground level on each post and then mark off pole hole positions at intervals indicated.

MATERIALS

Part	Quantity	Material	Length
POST	6	3 × 3in (75 × 75mm) S4S softwood	As required
POLE	21	1¼in (35mm) diameter doweling	66⅛in (1680mm)
SOFFIT BOARD	2	1 × 4in (25 × 100mm) S4S softwood	61½in (1560mm)
ROOF PANEL	2	½in (12mm) WBP plywood	31½ × 61½in (800 × 1560mm)
RIDGE BATTEN	1	2 × 3in (50 × 75mm) S4S softwood	61½in (1560mm)
SLIDE BASE	1	½in (12mm) WBP plywood	15¾ × 88½in (400 × 2250mm)
SLIDE SIDE	2	1 × 3in (25 × 75mm) S4S softwood	88½in (2250mm)
PLATFORM	1	¾in (19mm) WBP plywood	30 × 53½in (760 × 1360mm)
LOCATING BATTEN	2	1 × 2in (25 × 50mm) S4S softwood	30in (760mm)
TURNBUCKLE	4	Offcut of ⅜in (10mm) batten	Approx. ¾ × 2¾in (20 × 70mm)
SANDPIT SIDE	4	1 × 3in (25 × 73mm) S4S softwood	55⅛in (1400mm)
SWING SEAT	1	1 × 6in (25 × 150mm) S4S softwood	19¾in (500mm)

Also required: 1in (25mm) diameter rope, string and tape for swing; concrete for anchoring posts; 42 1½in (37mm) No. 10 woodscrews for "locking" poles to posts

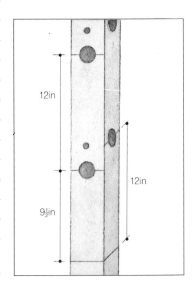

(150mm) deeper than the length of post to be buried, so in this case they will need to be 36in (900mm) deep. Place a 6in (150mm) layer of well-compacted hardcore in the bottom of each hole for drainage, and to prevent the posts rotting.

Lift the framework into the holes. Check that the assembly is level and plumb and that the marked lines are all at ground level. If necessary, remove the framework and adjust the hardcore as required.

Make up the concrete, using a mix of sand, aggregate, and cement in the ratio 1:5:1. Wear gloves to avoid the risk of burns. Pour the ingredients onto the mixing area, and turn it over with a shovel until it is a uniform gray color. Make a hole in the top of the pile and add a little water at a time.

Turn over the mix until the water is absorbed, then add more water and mix again to produce pliable concrete that is not too wet or sloppy.

Tip some of the concrete into a hole, add a few pieces of broken brick, and tamp them down with a stick so that there are no air pockets around the post. Fill the remaining 12in (300mm) of each hole with concrete, rounding it into a collar around the bases of the posts so that rainwater flows away.

Allow the concrete to set, then arrange the poles as required, inserting all the locking screws.

Bevel all the post tops to a 10 degree angle, using an adjustable bevel to mark off the angle accurately (fig. 2). The two pairs of posts that will support the roof are beveled in opposite directions to allow for the pitch of the roof (see **Climbing Frame Assembly, page 97**). The two uncovered end posts are also beveled to drain rainwater.

FITTING THE ROOF

Cut the two soffit boards to size. Along the underside of each, cut a $\frac{1}{4} \times \frac{1}{4}$in (6mm × 6mm) groove, $\frac{3}{8}$in (10mm) in from the edge. This encourages rainwater to drip away instead of rotting the wood.

Plane the top edge of each roof panel to an angle of 53 degrees and plane the bottom edge to an angle of 37 degrees (fig. 3). Use an

2 **Assembling the Poles**

Round over the ends of the poles and feed them through the holes in the posts so that they protrude by a maximum of 3in (75mm) at each end. Note top of post is beveled at 10 degrees.

3 **Making the Roof**

Above: **Angle ridge batten as marked so that it will fit in apex of roof.** *Below:* **Angle apex end of roof panel at 53 degrees and other end at 37 degrees. Glue and screw roof panels to ridge batten at apex.**

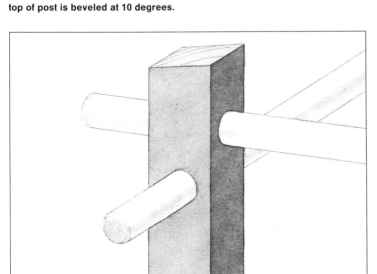

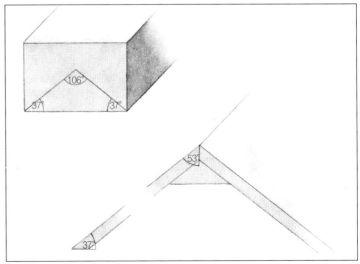

CLIMBING FRAME

adjustable bevel to mark the angles. Mark and cut the ridge batten as shown (fig. 3, page 101).

Fix the two roof panels at the apex by gluing and screwing down into the ridge batten. Use 1in (25mm) No. 8 woodscrews at approximately 12in (300mm) centers.

Place the assembled roof onto the soffits, check for alignment, then secure it by screwing upward through the soffits into the roof panel edges. Use 1½in (37mm) No. 8 screws at approximately 12in (300mm) centers (fig. 1).

SLIDE

Fasten the sides to the base with waterproof exterior adhesive and screw up through the base into the sides. Ensure that the edges are flush and use 1½in (37mm) No. 8 countersunk screws at 16in (400mm) centers.

Round over all the edges and the corners of the sides at both ends.

The slide is anchored to the pole using battens and notched turnbuckles (fig. 2). Cut two 1 × 2in (25 × 50mm) battens to the width of the slide. Screw the battens to the slide base, one at the top and the second about 1½in (38mm) down from the bottom of the first batten, so that the battens snugly enclose the pole of the climbing frame to which the slide will be attached.

Insert two screws into the lower batten, with about 1½in (38mm) of the threaded shank protruding. Saw off the screwheads and smooth the jagged points of the sawn ends.

Make two turnbuckles from ½in (12mm) plywood, cutting a small notch toward the bottom of one side so that they can be locked in place around the screws using a butterfly nut on each. Screw the turnbuckles to the top batten as shown (fig. 2), as tightly as possible, but remembering that they must pivot. This method of anchoring gives a secure fastening, but allows the slide to be taken down, removed, and packed away if required.

Fill the screw holes in the base. Sand all surfaces of the slide thoroughly to ensure there are no splinters, then apply several coats of exterior-grade varnish to them.

When anchoring the slide for use, it must not be any higher than the fourth pole up, otherwise the gradient will be too great. Place an impact-absorbent gym mat at the base, with the back edge held in place underneath the slide.

PLATFORM

The platform can be positioned across any opposite pairs of bars. If the slide is in use, then the platform must be positioned across bars corresponding to the slide level to provide a means of entrance.

Cut the ¾in (18mm) plywood to size. Glue and screw a 1 × 2in (25 × 50mm) locating batten to each of the shorter sides of the platform panel, flush with the edges. Use three 1½in (37mm) No. 8 countersunk screws on each side. Sand the platform to remove splinters.

Cut out four turnbuckles, about ¾ × 2¾in (20 × 70mm) from ⅜in (10mm) batten. Round over the ends and screw up into the underside of the locating battens, so that the turnbuckles pivot on the screws (fig. 3). Varnish all surfaces.

SANDPIT

Remove the turf from the area of the sandpit and simply lay down concrete paving slabs. Butt the edges closely together. If the lawn is uneven, level it with sand. Lay a sheet of thick polyethylene on top of the slabs so that no vegetation or insects creep into the sand.

Cut the sides of the sandpit to protrude 1in (25mm) beyond the posts at each end. Position each side piece against the inside face of two posts and mark off on the side where it meets the inner corner of the posts. Cut cross-lap joints on the longer side of these marks (fig. 4). Round over the top edges. Screw the sides to the posts using two 1½in (37mm) No. 8 countersunk screws at each end (fig. 5).

If you want a greater depth of sand in the pit, either use wider boards or excavate the lawn to the required depth and use boards of sufficient width to rise 3in (75mm) above ground level. Fill the pit with special fine-grade sand available from toy centers.

1 Fitting the Soffit Board
Screw soffit board down into top of post; then screw through board up into bottom edge of roof panel.

2 Fitting the Slide
Screw battens to the underside of the slide base so they enclose the pole. Screw turnbuckles to the top batten so that they pivot across to enclose sawn-off screws in lower batten and are held in place using butterfly nuts.

3 Fitting the Platform
Glue and screw battens to edges of short side of platform. Add turnbuckles to hold platform in place.

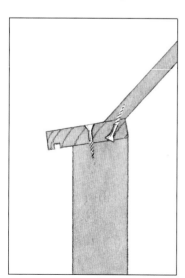

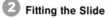
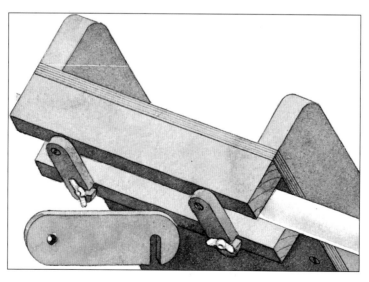

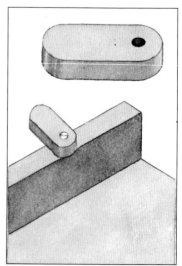

4 **Making the Sandpit Sides**
Mark the inside post corners on the sandpit sides and cut cross-lap joints to join the sides.

5 **Fitting the Sandpit Sides**
Screw the sandpit sides to the inside faces of the posts so that they protrude 1in (25mm).

6 **Adding a Swing**
Feed rope through holes in swing seat and knot tightly beneath. Make loop at top for pole to feed through.

SWING

Drill two holes at either end to take 1in (25mm) diameter rope. Round off the corners and sand the seat smooth. Thread the rope through each pair of holes and tightly knot each end. Wind string at the top to form a loop and knot it firmly.

Feed one end of the pole through the post at the highest position, through the rope loops, and through the opposite post. Center the swing between the posts, mark the rope positions, and remove the pole. Cut shallow V-shapes in the top of the pole at the rope positions, then feed it back in place. Insert the locking screws, position the ropes in the grooves, and screw or nail them in place. Varnish the seat.

If you prefer, you could suspend a tire from the rope instead.

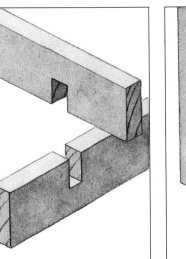

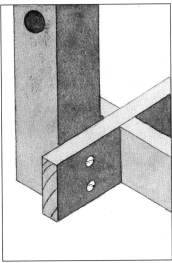

CART

Children are always fascinated by forms of transportation – things to ride in or push, things to move from place to place. This handsome wooden cart with its elegant tapering shafts, inspired by the shape of an Austrian hay-cart, has a basic simplicity which allows room for the imagination. Chariot or truck, carriage or wagon, it can be pulled or pushed, ridden in or filled with toys according to the games of the day.

Certain aspects of the design make this one of the more difficult projects in the book. The body of the cart tapers inward, which calls for some skill in the setting up and cutting of angles. Contrary to appearances, the curved shafts are not particularly hard to make; the shape can be easily cut out using a saber saw, although the final shaping of the shafts with a spokeshave introduces an element of craftsmanship. The wheels, of course, are bicycle wheels, finely engineered and remarkably cheap. Their elegant spokes are echoed in the design of the railed sides. Here, careful measurement and drilling are required to fit the dowels accurately.

The central seat can take two small children sitting side by side. Smartly painted, and with its gleaming wheels, the cart is light and easy to maneuver, and will prove as irresistible to play with as it is satisfying to make.

CART

This cart makes a handsome toy for playing with in the backyard. It is substantial enough to allow two small children to sit in it, but it would then require an adult to push it around. Softwood is relatively light and even quite small children will want to have a go at pushing the cart when it is unfilled; however, they will have difficulty maneuvering it, so it is most important that you supervise children when they play with this item. Stops could be fitted at both ends of the cart to limit the tipping action, especially when children are climbing in or out.

This cart is made to a traditional design using mostly S4S (smooth 4 sides) softwood, and two standard 24in (610mm) bicycle wheels. The side and end panels require 10in (255mm) wide, planed $1\frac{1}{4}$in (32mm) thick lumber which may not be readily available. If this is the case, either buy wider lumber – $1\frac{1}{4} \times 12$in (32 × 300mm) should be available – or buy two lengths of $1\frac{1}{4}$in (32mm) thick planed lumber to a suitable width (say two of $1\frac{1}{4} \times 6$in [32 × 150mm]) and join them together by rub-gluing and clamping them to make up the required width. Both of these alternatives can then be cut down to size.

You will also need the assistance of two helpers to watch and guide you as you drill the angled holes for the dowels that form the cart's sides. These have to be very accurately drilled in order to continue the splay of the cart.

TOOLS

WORKBENCH (fixed or portable)

STEEL MEASURING TAPE

MARKING GAUGE

TRY SQUARE

ADJUSTABLE BEVEL

PAIR OF DIVIDERS (or compasses)

SABER SAW

POWER DRILL

DRILL BITS – $\frac{1}{2}$in (12mm), plus various sizes for pilot holes

COUNTERSINK BIT

CIRCULAR SAW (or panel saw)

SMOOTHING PLANE (hand or power)

BELT SANDER or POWER FINISHING SANDER or HAND SANDING BLOCK

SCREWDRIVER

ROUTER

ROUNDING-OVER CUTTER or SPOKESHAVE

STRAIGHT CUTTER – $\frac{1}{2}$in (12mm) (or back saw and $\frac{1}{2}$in [12mm] chisel)

SASH CLAMPS

C-CLAMPS

MALLET

HACKSAW

METAL FILE

MATERIALS

Part	Quantity	Material	Length
SIDE	2	$1\frac{1}{4} \times 10$in (32 × 255mm) S4S (smooth 4 sides) softwood	44in (1120mm)
END PANEL	2	As above	$26\frac{3}{4}$in (680mm)
CENTRAL SUPPORT	1	1in (25mm) plywood	$7\frac{3}{4} \times 26\frac{3}{8}$in (195 × 670mm)
BASE SUPPORT BATTEN	4	1×1in (25 × 25mm) S4S (smooth 4 sides) softwood	Approx. $21\frac{3}{4}$in (550mm)*
BASE SLAT	18	1×2in (25 × 50mm) S4S (smooth 4 sides) softwood	Approx. $25\frac{1}{2}$in (650mm)*
SEAT SUPPORT BATTEN	2	$1\frac{1}{4} \times 1\frac{1}{4}$in (32 × 32mm) S4S (smooth 4 sides) softwood	As above*
SEAT	1	1×6in (25 × 150mm) S4S (smooth 4 sides) softwood	As above*
SHAFT	2	From $1\frac{1}{2} \times 9$in (38 × 225mm) joinery-grade S4S (smooth 4 sides) softwood	48in (1220mm)
TOP SIDE RAIL	2	1×2in (25 × 50mm) S4S (smooth 4 sides) softwood	47in (1190mm)
TOP END RAIL	2	As above	$31\frac{3}{4}$in (805mm)
DOWEL	52	$\frac{1}{2}$in (12mm) diameter doweling	$7\frac{1}{2}$in (190mm)

Also required: 2 bicycle wheels, 24in (610mm) in diameter, with hub assemblies; 2 galvanized angle joist straps (from building supply stores)

CART ASSEMBLY

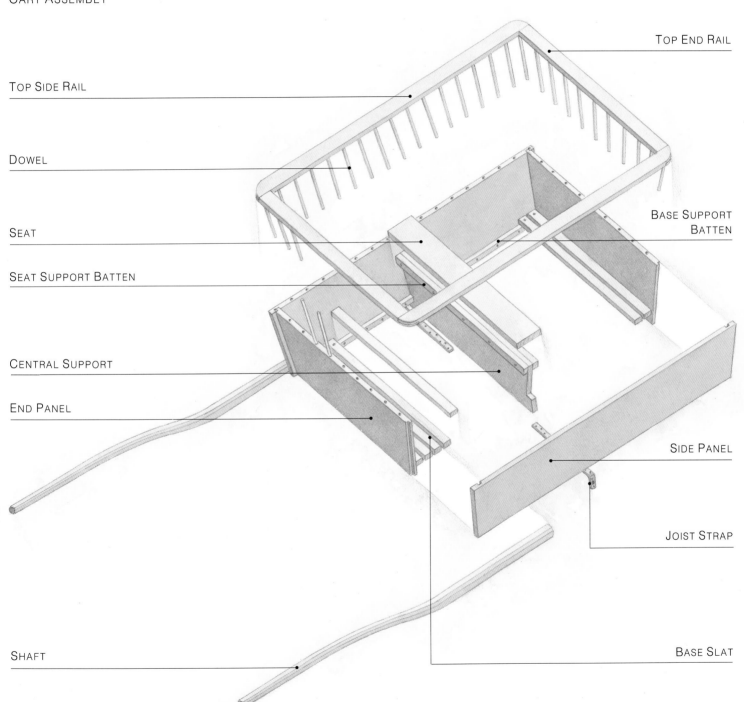

TOP END RAIL

TOP SIDE RAIL

DOWEL

SEAT

BASE SUPPORT
BATTEN

SEAT SUPPORT BATTEN

CENTRAL SUPPORT

END PANEL

SIDE PANEL

JOIST STRAP

SHAFT

BASE SLAT

CART

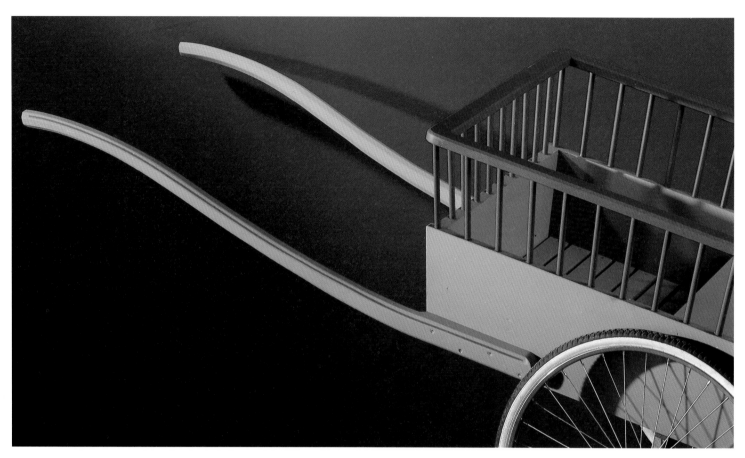

1 Shaping the Sides and Ends

Above: Angle ends by 10 degrees.
Below: Rout dados $1\frac{3}{8}$in (35mm) in from ends of side panels.

2 Rabbeting the End Panels

Above: Cut $\frac{1}{4} \times \frac{1}{2}$in (6 × 12mm) rabbets in end panels. *Below* Plan view of end rabbeted into side dado.

3 Shaping the Central Support

Above: Centrally position an end panel $1\frac{1}{2}$in (40mm) up from bottom edge of central support and draw around ends on to central support. *Below:* Cut around marked lines on support to leave protruding tongues at base.

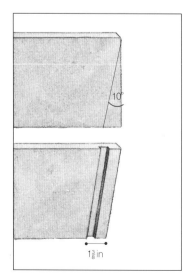

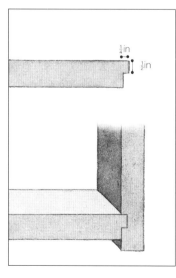

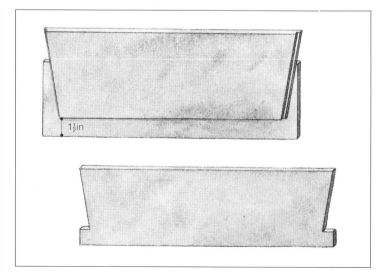

THE BASIC FRAME

The side and end panels of the cart all slope inward at the bottom. The end panels and central support slot into dados cut into the inside faces of the side panels.

Start by shaping the ends of the side and end panels. Using an adjustable bevel, mark a 10 degree angle on the ends of the panels from the top (fig. 1, above). Saw down these marked lines carefully.

On what will be the inside faces of the side panels, mark a line 1⅜in (35mm) in from, and parallel with, each angled end. Cut a dado ¼in (6mm) deep and ½in (12mm) wide against each of these lines (fig. 1, below). Use a router fitted with a guide fence and a ½in (12mm) straight cutter; alternatively, draw a second line, cut down it with a back saw and chisel out the waste.

On each end of the end panels rout or cut out a rabbet to give a tongue ¼in (6mm) long and ½in (12mm) wide so that the rabbets fit tightly into the dado in each of the side panels (fig. 2).

CENTRAL SUPPORT

On the central support, mark a line 1½in (40mm) up from the bottom edge along the full length of the panel and parallel with the bottom. Centrally position one of the end panels along this line, with the tongues face down. Mark the angles of the end panel's ends on the central support, remove the end panel, and saw down the marked lines to remove the waste, leaving the 1½in (40mm) deep sections protruding at the bottom (fig. 3).

The central support slots into dados cut midway along the side panels (fig. 4). Offer up the central support to the mid-point of a side panel. Mark the length and width of the dado required on the side panel. Remove the central support and accurately mark the dado, checking that its width is exactly the thickness of the central support. Mark a dado for the central support on the inside of the other side panel at its mid-point. Rout out or cut the dados to a depth of ¼in (6mm) in both of the side panels.

ASSEMBLING MAIN FRAME

Assemble the sides, ends, and central support using a waterproof woodworking adhesive. Ensure that the top and bottom edges are flush at the corners, and that the protruding sections on the central support are pushed up tight against the bottom edges of the sides (fig. 5).

Hold the assembly together with sash clamps placed across each end and, ideally, across the middle, or use webbing clamps right around the frame. Check that the assembly is square, then leave it until the adhesive is dry.

BASE

When the basic assembly is dry, the base can be fitted. Measure the space between the central support and the end panels, 1½in (40mm) up from the bottom and cut the four base support battens to this length. One edge and one end of each batten will need to be beveled at 10 degrees so that each batten fits neatly against the side panels (fig. 6, above). Then glue, screw, and

countersink each batten to the sides, with the top edge positioned 1½in (40mm) up from the bottom edge of the sides.

For the base slats, cut one length to fit tightly across the frame, resting on top of the support battens (fig. 6, below). This will require you to bevel the ends by 10 degrees (as before) to fit. When the first base slat has been cut to fit snugly, cut the remaining 17 slats to this length, with the saw blade set to the correct angle for the ends.

Space the slats equally so that there are nine on each side of the central support. Glue, screw, and countersink the slats down on to the support battens.

SEAT

Cut the two seat support battens to the length of the top edge of the central support, allowing for 10 degree beveled ends as before. Drill and countersink holes on the side and underside of each batten and glue and screw to the central support so that the top edges are flush (fig. 1, page 110).

4 Dado for Central Support
Mark height and width of central support midway along side panels. Rout dado to depth of ¼in (6mm).

5 Finished Assembly of the Basic Frame
Glue end panels and central support into dados cut into side panels. Ensure that corners and edges are flush, and that protruding tongues of central support are pushed up against bottom edges of side panels.

6 Fitting the Base
Above: **Bevel edge of batten by 10 degrees to abut side panels.** *Below:* **Screw base slats to support battens.**

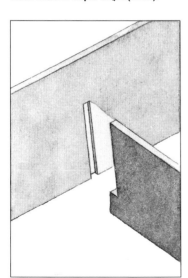

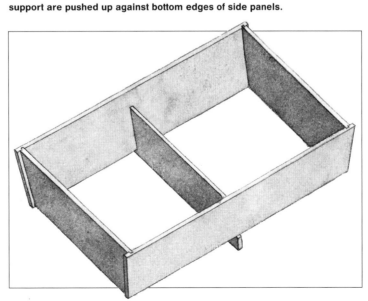

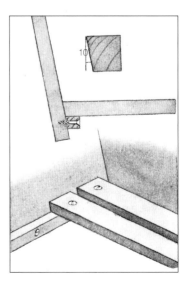

CART

Measure the width of the cart 1in (25mm) above the top of the central support and cut the seat to fit; do not forget that you will need to bevel both of the ends at 10 degrees. Place the seat in position and screw up through the battens into the seat to secure it (fig. 1).

Plane the top and bottom edges of the whole frame so they are perfectly horizontal.

SHAFTS

Cut both the shafts from a single piece of $1\frac{1}{2} \times 9$in (38×225mm) S4S (smooth 4 sides) joinery-grade softwood. Good-quality, knot-free lumber is absolutely essential here for strength; knots would severely weaken the shafts.

Draw sweeping curves on the softwood to its full length and width so the two shafts can be sequentially cut (fig. 2, above). Start the shaft at about $2\frac{1}{8}$in (55mm) wide, keeping straight for the first 10in (250mm) then curving and tapering to the thickness of the lumber, about $1\frac{3}{8}$in (34mm), at the other end. Repeat for the second shaft.

Cut out the shafts using a saber saw. Mark off the first 10in (250mm), which will be fixed to the cart, and round over the corners at the back end (fig. 2, below). Using a spokeshave, bevel all four corners all the way along each shaft. However, do *not* bevel the inner corners along the 10in (250mm) fixing section. The shafts will now be octagonal in cross section at the handle end. Sand the faces of the shafts smooth.

Glue and screw the shafts to the sides of the base frame, with the bottom edges of the shafts positioned $\frac{3}{8}$in (10mm) up from the bottom edges of the cart sides. Use four large screws in each shaft and countersink the screw holes.

TOP RAIL

The top side and top end rails are joined together with half-lap joints, which should be cut so that the side rails are lapping over the end rails (fig. 3, above). Cut the joints and glue them up using waterproof woodworking adhesive, holding each joint together with a C-clamp until the adhesive has set.

MARKING OUT DOWEL POSITIONS

Mark a center line along the top edges of the base frame sides and ends, and on the underside of the top rail. Where the center lines intersect are the centers of the four corner dowel positions.

Measure the distance between the centers of the corner holes along the top edges of the base frame and along the underside of the top rail. Divide these distances by 10 at the ends and by 16 at the sides. Set a pair of dividers or compasses to the calculated spacings to check there are no errors in the calculations, and mark the center points of the dowel hole positions. The spaces will be wider on the top frame than on the bottom one. Make sure they are all marked out accurately before drilling.

DRILLING DOWEL HOLES

The dowel holes must be drilled accurately at the same angles as the cart sides and ends. This requires the assistance of two people. With

the cart on a level surface, one person stands facing the side, and one facing the end. They can then eye up the drill as you work to ensure that the holes are splayed at the correct angle to follow the line of the cart. It will be easier if, as you drill each hole, you put a dowel in place (fig. 4). Put a length of insulation tape around the drill bit at a depth of $\frac{3}{8}$in (8mm) to ensure that all the holes are drilled to the same depth.

With the guidance of your helpers, repeat the procedure for the drilling of the top frame, which should be placed bottom side up on a flat surface. Again, insert the actual dowels as guidance for the correct alignment.

ASSEMBLING TOP FRAME

Check that all the dowels are exactly the same length. Put waterproof woodworking adhesive in each dowel hole in the base frame and in the top rail. Repeat this on top of the dowels and wriggle each one up in turn to locate them all halfway into the top rail frame. Gently tap the top frame down with a mallet so that all

① Fitting the Seat
Fit support battens along length of central support at top. Screw up through the battens into the seat.

② Shaping the Shafts
Above: **Mark out both of the shafts on a piece of $1\frac{1}{2} \times 9$in (38×225mm) S4S and cut out using a saber saw.** *Below:* **Round over the corners and edges of the back end and screw to sides.**

③ Shaping the Top Rail
Above: **Cut half lap joints so that side rails lap over end rails.** *Below:* **Round over the corners.**

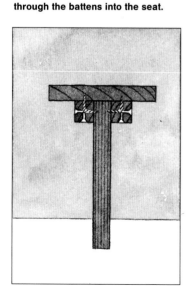

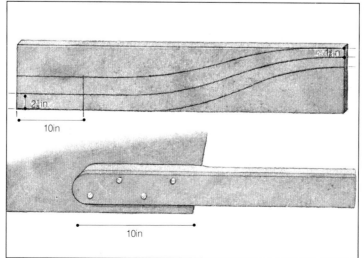

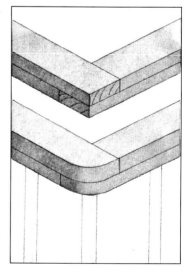

the dowels are fully home, top and bottom. Leave the assembly to dry.

Sand all the edges smooth, and, if required, plane them at an angle. Round off the corners of the top frame using a router fitted with a rounding-over cutter or using a spokeshave (fig. 3, below). Bevel the top outer edges.

FITTING THE WHEELS

Turn the cart upside down and cut the two galvanized angled joist straps to length using a hacksaw so that the two straps meet in the middle across the underside of the central support. The angles of the straps should protrude just beyond the outer ears of the central support to give a downstand of $2\frac{1}{2}$in (65mm) (fig. 5). Use a hacksaw to trim off any excess strap and round off straight edges and corners with a file. Screw the joist straps to the underside of the central support.

Drill a hole in the downstand for the axle of the bicycle wheel to fit through. Tighten the fixing nuts to hold the wheels in place on each side of the cart.

④ Drilling the Dowel Holes
Space dowel holes regularly along end and side panels. Drill holes at angle to follow line of cart frame.

⑤ Adding the Wheels
With the cart turned upside down, screw two joist straps to the bottom edge of the central support. Drill a hole in the downstand of each of the straps to take the axle of the bicycle wheel.

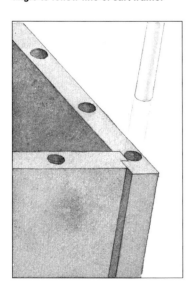

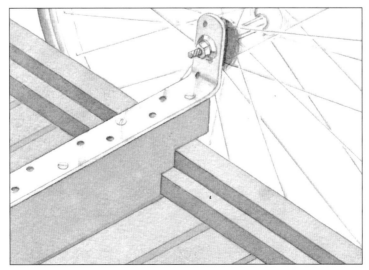

ROUND-THE-HOUSES GOLF

Here's an outdoor game for all ages which is simple to make and fun to play, and can be used on any lawn. The "targets" can be arranged in close proximity or spread wide apart to make things a little more difficult. Older players should be given a handicap to even chances.

The game consists of 18 "holes" of golf. The holes are completed by directing the golf ball through a doorway in a building, by driving the ball against a solid door so that it rebounds (as in the case of holes No. 4, No. 10, and No. 15), or by hitting a stake (holes No. 6, No. 9, and No. 13). Hole No. 11 incorporates an obstacle in the form of a ramp. After playing hole No. 10, the ball must be driven up the ramp and through the opening in the wall; once it has rolled down the other side, hole No. 12 can be played.

The game is laid out as shown (fig. 1). As can be seen, both the front and back of certain openings in the buildings are used as two holes. For example, hole No. 2 backs on to hole No. 17 and hole No. 5 backs on to hole No. 14. The course must be completed in numerical order, with each player taking one shot in turn. The player completing the course with the fewest number of strokes is the winner.

The game can be made more difficult by making each opening only slightly wider than the diameter of the ball being used.

The longer rows of houses are 4ft (about 1.2m) so the game can be stored away neatly indoors or in a shed when it is not in use.

To make the game, first mark out the outline and openings of the buildings on $\frac{3}{8}$in (9mm) exterior-grade plywood and cut them out using a saber saw or compass saw. Paint the houses with primer then gloss in any preferred colors, then paint on the hole numbers. The white decorative strips in our illustration were made by adding adhesive tape after the paint had dried.

1 Setting Out the Game

The houses are staked into the lawn following the plan below. Players negotiate a route through the "town" following the painted numbers on the houses (1–18). Note that some openings have numbers painted on both sides.

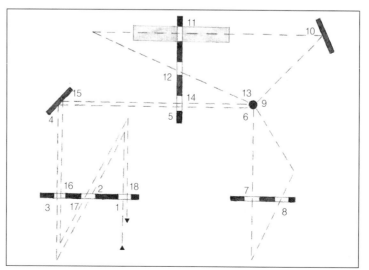

TOWN DRIVE

This brightly painted miniature town forms a "golf course" that is quick and easy to make.

The ramps leading up to and down from hole No. 11 measure $5\frac{1}{4} \times 16\frac{1}{2}$in (130 × 420mm). The ends on the ground should be pressed into the soil for stability.

The stake for targets No. 6, No. 9, and No. 13 is $\frac{7}{8} \times 6$in (22 × 400mm) exterior-grade plywood. The clubs are $1\frac{1}{4} \times 35\frac{1}{2}$in (28 × 900mm) softwood and are screwed to the "head" using countersunk 1in (25mm) No. 8 screws. Paint the clubs in bright colors, then decorate them with white adhesive tape.

The buildings can be wedged upright by driving thin stakes, front and back, into the ground. Make sure an adult supervises this.

WEATHER VANE

This unusual figure is not just an ornament but a weather vane too. It will amuse children and teach them something about wind direction.

The main body of the goose is made from $\frac{3}{4}$in (18mm) exterior-grade plywood, about $12 \times 31\frac{1}{2}$in (300 × 800mm). Cut parts from a full-scale pattern following the grid (fig. 1). Each square measures $\frac{3}{4} \times \frac{3}{4}$in (20 × 20mm).

Apart from the main body (A), you need to cut two of the trapezoid-shaped parts (B) and four wings (C). The wings are cut from $\frac{1}{8}$in (4mm) exterior-grade plywood and need to be exactly the same shape, so temporarily nail or clamp four pieces of plywood together, draw the outline on the top piece, and cut all four pieces together using a saber or compass saw.

The two wings on each side of the goose are set at an angle to each other to create a propeller shape. This is achieved by mounting each pair on to a $3\frac{5}{8}$in (90mm) long softwood wing block, $1\frac{3}{8}$in (35mm) square. A $\frac{1}{8}$in (4mm) wide diagonal slot is cut in each end of the block. The diagonals must be cut in opposite directions to give the propeller its necessary twist. Fit the wings in the slots using waterproof woodworking adhesive.

Parts B are glued and nailed to the sides of the body as indicated by the area (D). The short ends should face outward.

Drill a $\frac{1}{4}$in (6mm) hole, $3\frac{1}{4}$in (80mm) deep in the edge of the goose stomach at an 86 degree angle to take the axle. This is made from a piece of $\frac{1}{4}$in (6mm) diameter threaded bolt, 8in (200mm) long, and is tapped into the hole with a little waterproof adhesive added.

Drill two $\frac{1}{4}$in (5mm) diameter holes into short edges of parts B.

Paint all the parts white, allow to dry, then paint them black and gray.

Where the threaded bolt enters the stomach, tighten two nuts. Slide the bolt into a $\frac{3}{8}$in (9mm) diameter brass tube fitted into the pole that the goose is to perch on. Place a couple of washers below the nuts before putting the bolt in the tube and add a drop of oil now and then to ensure free movement.

Through each wing block, drill a $\frac{3}{8}$in (9mm) diameter hole and slip a length of brass tube through it. This acts as a lining and ensures the wing turns freely on the $\frac{1}{4} \times 2\frac{3}{4}$in (6 × 70mm) lag screw that secures it in position. Add a couple of washers to ensure the wings swivel freely.

Fit the pole to a post where it will get the full blast of the wind.

WEATHERING WELL

This handsome goose weather vane pivots around the brass tube according to the direction of the wind. The angled wings on either side also turn in the wind, for added interest.

① **Marking Out and Cutting the Parts for the Weather Vane**
Onto a $\frac{3}{4} \times \frac{3}{4}$in (20 × 20mm) grid, transfer the parts for the goose: the body (A), wing supports (B), and wings (C). Note how a threaded bolt encased in a brass tube protrudes up into the body of the goose.

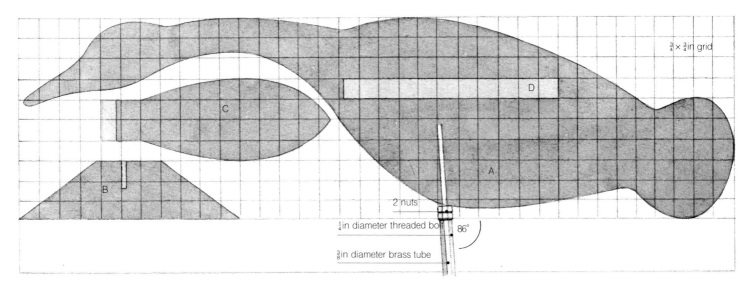

$\frac{3}{4} \times \frac{3}{4}$in grid

C

D

B

A

2 nuts

$\frac{1}{4}$in diameter threaded bolt   86°

$\frac{3}{8}$in diameter brass tube

Tools for Preparation

Bench stop and vise A vise is fitted to the underside of a bench, the jaws level with the bench top. The jaws are lined and topped with hardwood to protect the work and any tools being used. Some vises incorporate a small steel peg (a "dog") that can be raised above the main jaw level. This allows awkward pieces of wood to be clamped in position when used with a bench stop fitted at the opposite end of the bench.

Drill stand Enables a power drill to be used with extreme accuracy when, for example, dowel jointing. The hole will be perpendicular to the surface and its depth can be carefully controlled. The drill is lowered onto the work with a spring-loaded lever which gives good control.

Adjustable bevel This is a type of square used to mark out lumber at any required angle. The sliding blade can be locked against the stock by means of a locking lever and the blade can form any angle with the stock.

Marking gauge This is used to mark both widths and thicknesses with only a light scratch. The gauge comprises a handle, on which slides a stock bearing a steel marking pin which can be fixed at a precise point.

Mortise gauge Similar to a marking gauge, it has two pins, one fixed, one adjustable, to mark out both sides of a mortise at the same time.

Contour gauge This is also called a shape tracer or a scribing gauge. It comprises a row of steel pins or plastic fingers held in a central bar. When pressed against an object, like a base-board, the pins follow the shape of the object.

Utility knife Used to score a thin line for a saw or chisel to follow, ensuring a precise cut.

Miter box A simple open-topped wooden box which is used to guide saws into materials at a fixed 45° or 90° angle, to ensure an accurate cut.

Plumb bob and chalk Used to check or mark accurate vertical lines on walls. A plumb bob is simply a pointed weight attached to a long length of string. The string can be rubbed with a stick of colored chalk to leave a line on the wall.

Portable workbench A collapsible, portable workbench is vital for woodworking. It is light-weight and can be carried to the job, where it provides sturdy support. A portable bench is like a giant vise – the worksurface comprises two sections which can be opened wide or closed tightly according to the dimensions of the work and the nature of the task. It is used to hold large or awkward-shaped objects.

Scribing block To fit an item neatly against a wall (which is very unlikely to be completely flat), the item has to be "scribed" flat to the wall using a small block of wood and a pencil (*see* **Techniques, page 119**). A scribing block is simply a scrap of wood measuring about $1 \times 1 \times 1$in ($25 \times 25 \times 25$mm). The block is held against the wall, a sharp pencil is held against the opposite end of the block, and the block and the pencil are moved in a unit along the wall to mark a line on the item to be fitted. If you cut to this line, the item will then fit tightly against the wall.

Carpenter's level Used for checking that surfaces are horizontal or vertical. A 39in (1000mm) long level is a very useful all-around size. An aluminum or steel level will withstand knocks and can be I-girder or box-shaped in section. A 10in (250mm) carpenter's level is useful for working in confined spaces and can be used with a straight-edge over longer surfaces.

Steel measuring tape An 8ft (2.4m) or 15ft (5m) long, lockable tape (metal or plastic) is best, and one with a top window in the casing makes it easier to read measurements.

Steel rule Since the rule is made of steel, the graduations are indelible and very precise. A rule graduated on both sides in U.S. measure and metric is the most useful. The rule also serves as a precise straight-edge for marking cutting lines.

Straight-edge Can be made from a length of 1×2in (25×50mm) scrap wood. It is used in combination with a carpenter's level to tell whether a surface is flat and also for checking whether two points are aligned with each other.

Try square An L-shaped precision tool comprising a steel blade and stock (or handle) set at a perfect right angle to each other on both the inside and outside edges. Used for marking right angles and for checking a square.

Tools for Sharpening and Cutting

Chisels

Used to cut slots in wood or to pare off thin slivers. Some chisels may be used with a mallet. When new, a chisel's cutting edge must first be honed with an oilstone to sharpen it.
Mortise chisel Used for cutting deep slots.
Firmer chisel For general-purpose use.
Bench chisel Used in confined spaces.
Paring chisel Has a long blade for cutting deep joints or long dados.

Doweling jig Clamps onto a piece of work, ensuring that the drill is accurately aligned over the center of the dowel hole to be drilled. It also guides the drill vertically.

Drills

Hand drill For drilling holes for screws or for making large holes, particularly in wood. It will make holes in metal and is useful where there is no power source. A handle attached to a toothed wheel is used to turn the drill in its chuck.
Power drill These range from a simple, single-speed model (which will drill holes only in soft materials) to a multi-speed drill with electronic control. Most jobs call for something in between, such as a two-speed drill with hammer action.

Drill Bits

You will need a selection of drill bits in various sizes and of different types for use with a drill.
Countersink bit After a hole is drilled in wood, a countersink bit is used to cut a recess for the screwhead to sit in, so ensuring that it lies below the surface. Different types are available for use with a carpenter's brace or a power drill.
Brad-point bit Used to make dowel holes. The top has two cutting spurs on the side and a center point to prevent the bit from wandering off center.
Spade bit Used with a power drill. For maximum efficency the bit must be turned at high speed from about 1000 to 2000 r.p.m. It drills into cross grain, end grain, and man-made boards.
Masonry bit Has a specially hardened tungsten-carbide tip for drilling into masonry to the exact size required for a wall anchor. Special percussion drill bits are available for use with a hammer drill when boring into concrete.
Twist drill bit Used with a power drill for drilling small holes in wood and metal.

Power router   This portable electric tool is used to cut grooves, recesses, and many types of joints in lumber, and to shape the edge of long lumber battens. A range of cutting bits in different shapes and sizes is available, and when fitted into the router the bits revolve at very high speed (about 25,000 r.p.m.) to cut wood smoothly and cleanly. Although hand routers (which look like small planes) are available, all references to routers in this book are to power models.

SAWS

Circular saw   For cutting large pieces of lumber or sheets of board, as well as grooves and angles. The most popular size has a diameter of 7$\frac{1}{4}$in (187mm). Circular saws can be dangerous and must be used carefully. The piece of work must be held securely, supported on scrap battens, and the blade depth set so that it will not cut into anything below the work. The tool should be fitted with an upper and a lower blade guard.

Coping saw   Used to make curved or circular cuts. It has a narrow blade, which can be swiveled. When cutting, the blade can be angled so that the frame clears the edge of the work. Drill a hole close to the edge of the piece to be cut out, and thread the saw blade through the hole before reconnecting it to the handle.

Hacksaw   For cutting metal. A traditional hacksaw has a wooden handle and a solid metal frame. The blade is tensioned by a wing-nut. Modern hacksaws have a tubular frame which is adjustable for different lengths of blade.

Saber saw   More versatile than a circular saw, although not as quick or powerful. It cuts curves, intricate angles, and holes in a variety of materials. The best models offer variable speeds.

Compass saw   Has a narrow, tapered blade to cut holes and shapes in wood. A hole is drilled and the saw blade is inserted to make the cut.

Panel saw   A hand saw used for rough cutting rather than fine carpentry. It has a flexible blade of 20–26in (510–660mm).

Back saw   For cutting tenons, and for other delicate and accurate work. A back saw has a stiffened back and the blade is about 10–12in (250–300mm) long.

Surforms   Available in a range of lengths from approximately 6–10in (150–250mm), these rasps are useful for the initial shaping of wood. The steel blade has a pattern of alternating small teeth and holes through which waste wood passes, so that the teeth do not get clogged up.

HAND TOOLS

CLAMPS

Used for securing glued pieces of work in shape while they are setting.

C-clamp   Also called a frame clamp or fast-action clamp, it is important for our projects that the jaws of the clamp open at least 8in (200mm). The lumber to be held in the clamp is placed between the jaws which are then tightened by turning a thumb-screw, tommy bar, or other type of handle. With a fast-action clamp, one jaw is free to slide on a bar, and after sliding the jaw up to the workpiece, final tightening is achieved by turning the handle. To protect the work, scraps are placed between it and the jaws of the clamp.

Bar clamps   These employ a long metal bar, and are indispensable for holding together large frameworks, although you can improvise in some cases by making a rope tourniquet. This consists of a piece of rope which is tied around the object, and a length of stick to twist the rope and so cramp the frame tightly.

Band cramp   The webbing, like narrow seat belt-type material, is looped around the frame, pulled as tight as possible by hand, and then finally tightened by means of a screw mechanism or ratchet winder.

HAMMERS

Claw hammer   The claw side of the head of the hammer is used to extract nails from a piece of work, quickly and cleanly.

Cross-peen hammer   The peen is the tapered section opposite the flat hammer head, and it is used for starting off small brads and tacks.

Pin hammer   A smaller version of the cross-peen, this is useful for light work.

Mallet   Most commonly used to strike mortise chisels. The tapered wooden head ensures square contact with the object being struck.

Metal file   Gives a metal edge the required shape and finish. Most files are supplied with a removable handle which can be transferred to a file of a different size. Flat or half-round files (one side flat, the other curved) are good general-purpose tools.

Nailset   Used with a hammer to drive nails and brads below the surface so that they are hidden and the holes can then be filled.

Orbital sander   This gives a fine, smooth surface finish to wood. A gritted sanding sheet is fitted to the sander's base plate. Sheets are graded from coarse to fine, and the grade used depends on the roughness of the surface to be sanded. Always wear a mask when using one.

Paintbrushes   A set of paintbrushes for painting and varnishing should comprise three sizes – 1$\frac{1}{2}$in (37mm), 3in (75mm) and 4in (100mm). A better finish is always achieved by matching the size of the brush to the area you are painting.

PLANES

Block plane   Held in the palm of the hand, it is easy to use for small work and beveling edges.

Power plane   Finishes lumber to precise dimensions. A one-hand model is lightweight and can be used anywhere, whereas the heavier two-hander is intended for workbench use. A power plane will also cut bevels and rabbets.

Smoothing plane   A general-purpose hand-held plane for smoothing and straightening surfaces and edges. The plane is about 10in (250mm) long and its blade 2–2$\frac{1}{2}$in (50–60mm) wide. The wider the blade the better the finish on wide lumber. There is a fine adjustment for depth of cut and a lever for lateral adjustment.

Sanding block and sandpaper   A sanding block is used with sandpaper to finish and smooth flat surfaces. The block is made of cork, rubber, or softwood and the sandpaper is wrapped around it. Make sure in doing so that the paper is not wrinkled. Coarse paper is used for a rough surface and fine paper for finishing.

Screwdrivers   Come in many shapes and sizes, the main differences being the type of tip, the length, and the shape of the handle.

Ideally, you should have a range of screwdrivers for dealing with all sizes of screws. Ratchet models, which return the handle to its starting point, are the easiest to operate.

Wrench   A wrench is required for tightening carriage bolts. If the correct-size open-ended or ring wrench is not available, any type of adjustable wrench may be used.

Spokeshave   This allows curved edges to be shaped. Models with flat faces are intended for convex surfaces, while those with round faces smooth concave curves.

Materials

Timber and Boards

Lumber is classified in two groups – softwoods and hardwoods. Softwoods come from evergreen trees and hardwoods from deciduous trees. Check your lumber for defects before buying it. Avoid wood that is badly cracked or split, although you need not be concerned about fine surface cracks since these can be planed, sanded, or filled. Do not buy warped wood, as it will be impossible to work with. Check for warping by looking along the length of a board to see if there is any bowing or twisting.

When you get your wood home, condition it for about ten days. As the wood will have been stored in the open air at the yard, it will be "wet." Once indoors, it dries, shrinks slightly, and will warp unless stored flat on the ground. If you build with wood as soon as you get it home, your structure could run into problems later as the wood dries out. To avoid warping and aid drying, stack boards in a pile, with scraps of wood placed between each board to allow air to circulate. This will lower the moisture content to about 10 percent and condition the wood for use.

Wood for outdoor projects must be protected from rot and insect attack. It can be bought pre-treated with preservative, but this is expensive; alternatively, you can buy untreated wood and treat it, as soon as possible, with a water-based preservative. Pay special attention to end grain and to posts that will be buried below ground – these should stand in pots of preservative for a few days.

Softwood Softwood is much less expensive than hardwood and is used in general building work. Softwood is sold either by the *lineal* foot or the *board* foot. The former is based on the length of a piece of wood – for example, 8ft of 1 by 2 (1×2in [25×50mm]). The board foot is calculated by multiplying thickness (in inches) by width (in feet) by length (in feet) – so, 10ft of 1 by 6 would be 5 board feet: 1in $\times \frac{1}{2}$ft (6in) $\times$ 10ft.

It is important to remember that standard softwood sizes refer to sawn sizes – that is, how it is sawn at a mill. Sawn lumber is *not* suitable for the projects in this book – all the wood needs to have been planed. Such wood is referred to as S4S (smooth 4 sides), and, since planing takes a little off each face, it is $\frac{1}{4}-\frac{3}{4}$in (6–18mm) smaller in width and thickness than stated. Standard sizes should, therefore, be thought of as rough guides rather than exact measurements.

Hardwood Expensive and not as easy to obtain as softwoods. In home woodwork, it is usually confined to moldings and beadings, which are used to give edges a neat finish.

Boards Mechanically made from wood and other fibers, they are versatile, relatively inexpensive, made to uniform quality, and available in large sheets. All boards are made in 4×8ft (1220×2440mm) sheets. You need to know the advantages of each type of board before making your choice.

Hardboard The best known of all fiberboards. Common thicknesses are $\frac{1}{8}$in, $\frac{3}{16}$in, and $\frac{1}{4}$in (3mm, 5mm, and 6mm). As hardboard is weak and has to be supported on a framework, it is essentially a material for paneling.

MDF (medium-density fiberboard) A good, general-purpose building board. It is highly compressed, does not flake or splinter when cut, and leaves a clean, hard-sawn edge that does not need to be disguised as do other fiberboards. It also takes a very good paint finish, even on its edges. Thicknesses range from around $\frac{1}{4}-1\frac{3}{8}$in (6–35mm).

Particleboard Made by binding wood chips together under pressure, it is rigid, and fairly heavy. Particleboard is strong when reasonably well supported, but sawing it can leave an unstable edge and can blunt a saw. Ordinary screws do not hold well in particleboard; it is best to use twin-thread screws. Most grades of particleboard are not moisture-resistant and will swell up when wet. Thicknesses range from $\frac{1}{4}-1\frac{1}{2}$in (6–40mm), but $\frac{1}{2}$in, $\frac{3}{4}$in, and 1in (12mm, 18mm, and 25mm) are common.

Particleboard is widely available with the faces and edges veneered with natural wood, PVC, melamine, or plastic laminates.

Plywood Made by gluing thin wood veneers together in plies (layers) with the grain in each ply running at right angles to that of its neighbors. This gives it strength and helps prevent warping. The most common boards have three, five, or seven plies. Plywood is graded for quality: N is perfect, followed by A, B, C, and D in decreasing order of quality. Usual thicknesses of plywood are $\frac{1}{8}$in, $\frac{1}{4}$in, $\frac{1}{2}$in, and $\frac{3}{4}$in (3mm, 6mm, 12mm, and 18mm). WBP (weather and boil proof) grade board must be used for exterior work.

Lumber core Made by sandwiching natural lumber strips between wood veneers, the latter usually of Far Eastern redwood or plain birch. Although plain birch is a little more expensive than redwood, it is of a much better quality. Lumber core is very strong, but can leave an ugly edge when sawn, making edge fixings difficult. Lumber core is graded in the same way as plywood and common thicknesses are $\frac{1}{2}$in, $\frac{3}{4}$in, and 1in (12mm, 18mm, and 25mm).

Tongue-and-groove boarding Also called match boarding, or matching, this is widely used for cladding frameworks. The boarding has a tongue on one side and a slot on the other side. The tongue fits into the slot of the adjacent board; this join expands and contracts according to temperature and humidity without cracks opening up between boards. Some boards have a decoration, most commonly a beveled edge forming a V-joint, hence tongued, grooved and V-jointed (TGV) boarding.

Adhesives and Fillers

Adhesives Modern types are strong and efficient. If they fail, it is because the wrong adhesive is being used or the manufacturer's instructions are not followed carefully. For all general indoor woodworking, use an aliphatic resin (yellow woodworker's) glue – all glue manufacturers produce their own brand. For outdoor woodworking, you must always use either a synthetic resin adhesive that is mixed with water (this has gap-filling properties, so is useful where joints are not cut perfectly) or a two-part epoxy resin adhesive where the parts are applied separately to the surfaces being joined.

Fillers If the wood is to be painted over, use a standard cellulose filler – the type used for repairing cracks in walls. This filler dries white and will be evident if used under any other kind of finish. When a clear finish is needed, fill cracks and holes with a commercial wood filler or stopping. These are thick pastes and come in a range of wood colors. It is best to choose a color slightly paler than the surrounding wood, since fillers tend to darken when the finish is applied. Some experimentation may be needed, using a waste piece of matching wood.

In fine work, a grain filler is used to stop the final finish sinking into the wood. This is a paste, thinned with white spirit, and then rubbed into the surface. It is supplied in a range of wood shades.

FINISHES

The choice of finish is determined by whether the wood or board is to be hidden, painted, or enhanced by a protective clear finish.

Paint A high-quality latex semi-gloss or an oil-based enamel paint are suitable for wood, and are applied after a primer. Oil-based paints wash better and last longer, but latex paints are easier to use and quicker drying. Be sure to choose a primer with a similar composition as your topcoat. Do *not* use "old paints" you have around the house that may have been manufactured prior to February 1978 (when the 0.6% lead limitation went into effect) because they may contain a dangerous level of lead. In addition, check the label on the paint can to make sure the manufacturer does not recommend against using the paint on children's items such as cribs.

Preservative Unless lumber for use outdoors has been pressure-treated, you must coat it thoroughly with preservative. Modern water-based preservatives are harmless to plant life. They are available in clear, green, and a number of wood colors according to the finish you want.

Varnish Normally applied by brush, varnish can also be sprayed on. It is available as a gloss, satin, or matt finish, all clear. However, varnish also comes in different colors, so that you can change the color of the wood and protect it simultaneously. Do not allow children in the room when you are working with varnish, paints, and other solvent-based materials: it can be toxic to inhale the fumes. If possible, do this work outdoors. If not, open all windows and have an active ventilation system going, such as a fan. For outdoor use, always use an exterior-grade varnish or a yacht varnish.

FASTENINGS

The choice of fastening depends on the size and weight of the materials being fastened.

Battens A general term used to describe a narrow strip of wood used for a variety of purposes. The usual sizes are 1 × 1in (25 × 25mm) or 1 × 2in (25 × 50mm).

Battens can be screwed to a wall to serve as bearers for shelves or they can be fitted in a framework on a wall, with boards mounted over them to form a new "wall."

Dowels Used to make framework joints or to join boards edge-to-edge or edge-to-face.

Hardwood dowels are sold in diameters ranging from $\frac{1}{4}$–$\frac{3}{8}$in (6–10mm). Generally speaking, dowel lengths should be about one-and-a-half times the thickness of the boards being joined.

Dowels are used with adhesive, and when the joint is complete, it is important to allow any excess adhesive to escape from the joint. Dowels with fluted (finely grooved) sides and beveled ends will help this process. If you have plain dowels, make fine sawcuts along the length and bevel the ends yourself.

NAILS

Common nails With large, flat, circular heads, these are used for strong joins where frames will be covered, so that the ugly appearance of the nails does not matter.

Annular threaded nails Used where really strong fastenings are required.

Round finishing nails Used when the finished appearance is important. The heads of these nails are driven in flush with the wood's surface or countersunk so they are unobtrusive. They should be used when nailing a thin piece of wood to a thicker piece and there is a risk of splitting the wood.

Brads For fastening thin panels, these have unobtrusive heads that can be driven in flush with the wood's surface or punched below it.

Masonry nails For fixing lumber battens to walls as an alternative to screws and anchors.

SCREWS

All types of screws are available with conventional slotted heads or Phillips heads. The latter are best to use with an electric screwdriver.

For most purposes, screws with countersunk heads are ideal as the head lies flush with the surface after insertion. Round-head screws are for fastening metal fittings such as door bolts, which have punched-out rather than countersunk screw holes. Ovalhead screws are used where a neat appearance is important.

Wood screws These have a length of smooth shank just below the head. This produces a strong clamping effect, but there is a possibility of the unthreaded shank splitting the wood.

Twin-thread screws Less likely to split wood than wood screws. Except for larger sizes, they are threaded along their entire length, giving an excellent grip in lumber and board. The best types are zinc-plated, and so rust-resistant.

Lag screws For heavy-duty fixings when making frameworks requiring a strong construction. The screws have square or hexagonal heads and are turned with a wrench. A washer is used to prevent the head cutting into the lumber.

Wall anchors Use a masonry drill bit to drill a hole which matches the size of screw being used (a No. 10 bit with a No. 10 screw, for example). Insert the anchor in the hole, then insert the screw through the object being fitted and into the anchor. Tighten the screw for a secure fitting.

Solid wall fastenings The method of fitting to a solid brick or block wall is to use a wall anchor. Traditional fiber wall anchors have been superseded by plastic versions which accept a range of screw sizes, typically from No. 8 to No. 12.

Stud wall fastenings To guarantee a secure fitting for stud walls, you should locate the lumber uprights which form the framework of the wall and drive screws into them. If you want to attach something heavy and the lumber uprights are not in the required position, then you *must* fit horizontal battens to the lumber uprights.

Cavity-wall fastenings Used on hollow walls, which are constructed from plasterboard partition or lath and plaster and are found in modern and old houses respectively. There are many types of these fixtures including spring toggle, gravity toggle, and nylon toggle, and nearly all of them work on the same principle: expanding wings open up to grip the back of the wall, securing the fastening.

Wall anchor bolt Similar to an anchor, but with its own heavy-duty machine screw, this is used for heavier objects where a more robust wall fastening is required. You need to make a much larger hole in the wall, typically $\frac{3}{8}$in (10mm) in diameter. The anchor sleeve expands as the bolt is tightened.

Magnetic catches There must be perfect contact between the magnet fitted to the cabinet frame and the striker plate which is fitted to the door. The other important factor is the pulling power of the magnet – on wardrobe doors an 11–13lb (5–6kg) "pull" will keep the door shut.

Magnetic push latches are also useful. Push on the door inwards and it springs open just enough to be grasped and fully opened by the fingers.

TECHNIQUES: SAWING AND CUTTING

MEASURING AND MARKING SQUARE

Mark the cutting lines lightly with a hard pencil first, and then use a utility knife in conjunction with a straight-edge or try square along a steel rule to create a sharp, splinter-free line on the lumber.

To mark lumber square, use a try square with the stock (handle) pressed against a flat side of the lumber, called the face side or face edge. Mark a line along the square, using a knife in preference to a pencil, then use the square to mark lines down the edges from the face mark. Finally square the other face side, checking that the lines join up right around the lumber (fig. 1).

BRACING

Bracing is used to hold a frame or structure square, with the corners at perfect right angles (fig. 2).

Try square method Nail a batten into one rail, pull into square by using a try square, and then nail the batten into the adjacent rail.

SAWING AND CUTTING

Cross-cutting to length by hand Hold the lumber firmly with the cutting line (see **Measuring and marking square**, above) overhanging the right-hand side of the work-bench (if you are right-handed). With the saw blade held vertical and the teeth on the waste side of the cutting line, draw the handle back to start the cut. To prevent the saw jumping out of place, as you begin work hold the thumb joint of the other hand against the side of the saw blade (fig. 3).

Rip cutting by hand With the piece of lumber or board supported at about knee height, draw back the saw handle to start the cut as described above. Then saw down the waste side of the cutting line, exerting pressure on the down cut only. If the saw blade wanders from the line, cramp the edge of a lumber batten exactly above the cutting line on the side of the lumber or board to be retained, and saw along it, using the batten as a guide (fig. 5).

Using a portable power saw If the cutting line is only a short distance from a straight edge, adjust the saw's fence so that when it is run along the edge of the lumber, the blade will cut on the waste side of the cutting line (fig. 4, above). If the lumber or board is wide, or the edge is not straight, clamp a batten to the surface of the lumber or board so that the saw blade will cut on the waste side of the line when run along the batten (fig. 4, below).

Ensuring a straight cut When cutting panels or boards using a power circular saw or saber saw, the best way to ensure a straight cut is to clamp a guide batten to the surface of the work, parallel with the cutting line, so that the edge of the saw sole plate can be run along the batten. The batten position is carefully adjusted so that the saw blade cuts on the waste side of the cutting line. Depending on which side of the cutting line the batten is clamped, when using a circular saw, it is possible that the motor housing will foul the batten or C-clamps used to

hold the panel in place. In this case, replace the batten with a wide strip of straight-edged plywood clamped to the work far enough back for the motor to clear the clamps.

CUTTING A CIRCLE

With a saber saw Mark the circle on the face of the panel. If you do not have a compass, a good make-shift alternative can be made with a loop of string pivoted on a drawing pin at the center of the circle. Hold a pencil vertically in the loop at the perimeter to draw the circle.

In order to have a neat, splinter-free cutting edge, carefully score around the marked cutting line using a mat knife.

To start the cut, drill a hole about $\frac{3}{8}$in (10mm) in diameter just on the inside of the marked circle. Insert the saber saw blade through this hole and start the cut from this point, sawing carefully just on the waste side of the cutting line. By scoring the cutting line first using a utility knife, it will be easier to follow the line of the circle and get a smooth finished edge (fig. 6).

① Marking Lumber to Length and Square All Around
Mark across the face of the wood with a utility knife held against a try square blade. Move knife around corners and mark sides, and finally mark other side to join up the lines.

② Bracing a Frame Square
Nail a batten across a corner of the frame so that a 3-4-5 shape triangle is formed.

③ Cross-cutting to Length
Hold the lumber firmly. Steady the saw blade with the thumb joint as you start to saw.

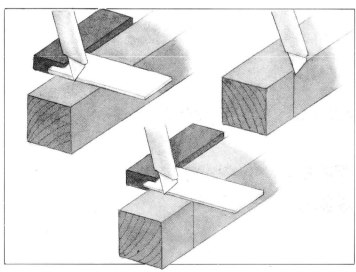

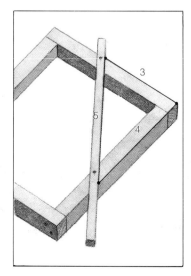

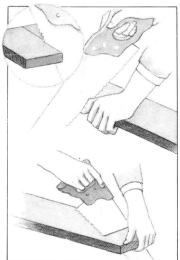

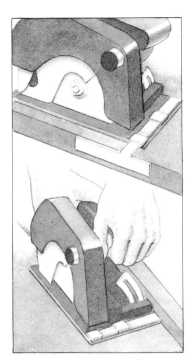

4 **Straight Power-Saw Cutting**
Top: **Use the rip fence of the saw if cutting near the edge of the piece of lumber.** *Above:* **Cutting alongside the guiding batten.**

5 **Straight Rip-cutting**
Clamp a straight batten alongside the cutting line and saw beside the batten. A wedge holds the cut open.

With a coping saw Mark out the circle, score the cutting line, and drill a hole about $\frac{3}{8}$in (10mm) in diameter just on the inside of the circle. Disconnect the blade from one end of the frame, pass the blade through the hole, and reconnect it to the frame. It will be best to clamp the piece of work vertically when cutting the circle. The blade can be turned in the frame to help the frame clear the piece of work, but even so, with a coping saw you will be restricted in exactly how far you are able to reach away from the piece of work. If the circle is positioned some way from the edge of the piece of board or lumber, use a compass or saber saw to cut it.

With a compass saw A compass saw has a stiff, triangular pointed saw blade attached to a simple handle. A very useful compass saw blade is available that can be simply fitted into a regular knife handle.

Because this type of saw has no frame, it is ideal for cutting circles and other apertures, like keyholes, anywhere in a panel.

6 **Using a Power Saber Saw**
For a straight cut clamp a batten alongside line. Cut a circle by following a marked outline.

Preparation of the circle for cutting is the same as for a coping saw. When cutting with a compass saw, keep the blade vertical and make a series of rapid, short strokes without exerting too much pressure (fig. 7).

CUTTING CURVES

The technique is basically the same as for cutting a circle, except that there will be no need to drill a hole in order to start the cut. You can use a saber saw, coping saw, or compass saw to make the cut. A coping saw is ideal for making this type of cut because most of the waste can be removed with an ordinary hand saw; you will be cutting close to the edge of the wood, so the saw frame will not get in the way (fig. 7, below).

PLANING

By hand Make sure that the plane blade is sharp and properly adjusted. Stand to one side of the work with feet slightly apart so you are facing the work. Plane from one end of the work to the other, starting the cut with firm pressure on the leading hand, transferring it to both

7 **Cutting Circles by Hand**
1: **Drill a small hole and cut circle using a compass saw;** *2:* **Making cut with a coping saw.**

hands, and finally to the rear hand as the cut is almost complete. Holding the plane at a slight angle to the direction of the grain may improve the cutting action.

With a power plane Remove loose clothing, and wear goggles and a dust mask. Clamp the work in place. Start the plane and turn the adjuster knob to set the depth. Start with a shallow cut and increase the depth if necessary.

Stand comfortably to one side of the work and, holding the plane with two hands, set it into the work at one end and pass it over the surface to the other end. When you have finished, switch off and make sure the blades stop spinning before resting the plane down with the cutting depth at zero.

SCRIBING

Scribing fillets are thin slats of wood used to fill the space between a built-in unit and the side walls. In this book they are used with the Swing-door Wardrobe if it is built-in.

House walls are rarely square, so for a neat finish, make the unit as a free-standing item about 2in (50mm) smaller than the width of the alcove at its narrowest point; then, after fitting the unit into place, scribe (shape) fillets into the gaps between the unit and the walls.

Before fitting the unit into place between the side walls of the alcove, screw 1 × 1in (25 × 25mm) vertical battens to each side of the unit. The battens should extend to the full height of the unit and should be set 2in (50mm) back from the front edge of the unit. A fillet, made from a strip of $\frac{1}{4}$in (6mm) plywood, is scribed to the outline of the wall surface and neatly fills the space between the unit and the wall. It is pinned in place to the batten and any small gaps are filled with filler before the fillet is painted to match the wall color. Setting the unit back in this way ensures a neat finish.

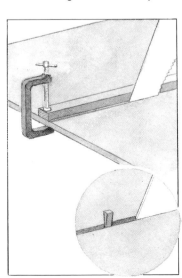

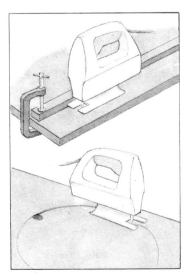

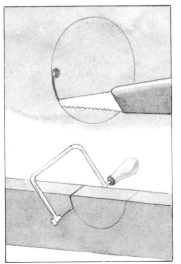

Techniques: Wall Fastenings

To scribe the fillet, hold a 3–4in (75–100mm) wide piece of the $\frac{1}{4}$in (6mm) plywood against the front face of the unit and press the edge against the side wall. Where the gap is widest, pull the fillet back so the gap between the edge of the fillet and the wall is 1in (25mm). Hold a pencil against a 1in (25mm) wide block and move the pencil along the wall to draw a cutting line along the fillet that follows the wall profile. Cut the edge of the fillet to this line. Move the fillet back against the wall and mark a straight line on the fillet to coincide with the edge of the unit. Cut the opposite edge of the fillet to this line and press the fillet in place. To secure, pin through the fillet into the fixing battens (fig. 1).

Cutting Grooves

With a router Use a straightsided router bit set to the depth required. Ideally, the bit should be the exact width of the groove. Otherwise, use a smaller router bit and cut the groove in two or more goes. Make the cut along the waste side with a batten clamped in place as a guide.

Drilling

To minimize the risk of splitting, drill pilot and clearance holes.

The **clearance hole** in the lumber should be slightly smaller in diameter than the screw shank.

The **pilot hole** to receive the screw should be about half the diameter of the clearance hole. The hole depth should be slightly less than the length of the screw.

To ensure that the screwheads lie level with the surface, use a counter-sink drill bit.

Drilling vertical holes To ensure vertical holes mount the drill in a stand (fig. 2). If this is not possible, stand a try square on edge so that its stock is resting on the work alongside the drilling position, and the blade is pointing up in the air. Use this as a sighting guide and line up the drill as close as possible with the square to ensure the drill is vertical (fig. 3). It is helpful if an assistant can stand back and sight along the drill and square to ensure the drill is straight.

Screwing

When screwing one piece of wood to another ensure that half of the screw penetrates through the bottom piece of wood. Its thickness should not exceed one-tenth of the width of the wood into which it has to be inserted. Keep screws at a distance of five times their shank diameter from the side edge of the wood, and ten times the shank diameter from its end.

Nailing

The correct length of nail to use is two-and-a-half to three times the thickness of the lumber being joined. However, check that the nail will not pierce right through two pieces being joined. Wherever possible nail through the thinner piece of wood into the thicker piece.

Nails grip best if driven in at an angle ("skew nailing," fig. 5). A row of nails is driven in at opposing angles to each other. Framework joints are usually held in by skew nailing. Clamp or nail a block of wood temporarily against one side of the vertical piece to stop it sliding as the first nail is started.

To prevent wood from splitting, blunt the points of the nails by hitting them with a hammer before driving them home. Blunt nails will cut through lumber fibers neatly, while pointed nails are more likely to push the fibers apart like a wedge.

Fastening

Solid wall The normal fastening for a solid wall is a woodscrew and plastic or fiber anchor. Before drilling the fixing hole, check with a metal detector that there are no pipes or cables hidden below the surface. Drill the holes for the wall anchor with a masonry drill bit in an electric drill. The anchor packing will indicate the drill size to use. The screw should be long enough to go through the fitting and into the wall by about 1in (25mm) if the masonry is exposed, and by about 1$\frac{3}{8}$in (35mm) if fixing into a rendered wall.

If the wall crumbles when you drill into it, mix up a cement-based anchoring compound (available from home improvement stores).

1 **Marking and Cutting a Scribing Fillet**
Left: Screw battens to unit sides, set back from front. *Middle:* Hold scribing fillet 1in (25mm) away from side wall at widest point and use pencil and block to follow wall profile. *Right:* Cut fillet to this line to fit against wall.

2 **Drilling Vertical Holes**
With a drill stand, not only will the drill bit be held vertical, but the depth is accurately controlled.

3 **Freehand Drilling Guide**
When drilling it can be helpful to stand a try square alongside the drill to ensure accuracy.

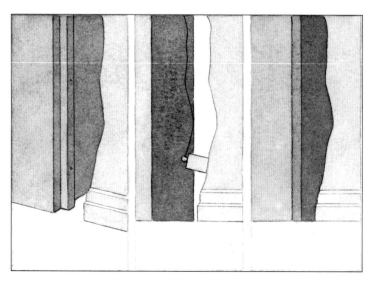

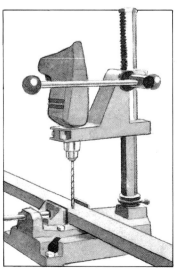

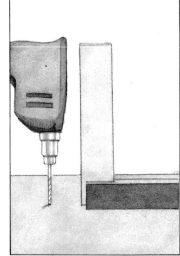

Turn back the screw about half a turn before the compound sets. When it is hard, the screw is removed and a fastening made.

If your drill sinks easily into the wall once it has penetrated the rendering, and a light gray dust is produced from the hole, you are fixing into lightweight building blocks. In this case, special winged anchors should be used.

To make a quick, light-to-medium weight fastening, a masonry nail can be used. Choose a length that will penetrate the material to be fixed, and pierce an exposed masonry wall by $\frac{5}{8}$in (15mm) or a rendered wall by about 1in (25mm).

Lath and plaster For a strong fastening, screw directly into the main vertical studding timbers to which the laths are nailed. You can find these studs with a metal detector (see **Stud wall**, below).

For a lightweight fastening you can screw into the wood laths. These can be located by probing with a pointed implement such as a awl. Then insert a twin-thread wood-screw. For medium-to-heavyweight fastenings into lath and plaster, drill between the laths and use a cavity-wall fastening suitable for lath and plaster, such as a spring toggle, gravity toggle, or nylon toggle.

Stud wall For a strong fastening into a gypboard-covered stud wall, make a screw fastening directly into the vertical studs. You can find these by tapping the wall to check where it sounds most dense, and then probing these areas with a pointed implement until a firm background is found. By drilling about 1in (25mm) to the farther side of this mark, the center of the stud will be found and a screw can be inserted.

To avoid making unnecessary holes, a metal detector can be used. Move it over the wall to locate a pattern of nail fixings and mark this on the surface. Vertical rows indicate a stud. Alternatively, use an electronic stud and joint detector. This is moved over the surface to detect a change in density between the different construction materials. A change indicates a stud.

If a fastening cannot be made into a stud, a lighter fastening can be made into gypboard by using a specially designed fitting. Follow the manufacturer's instructions.

Cavity wall Cavity walls comprise a solid inner leaf of bricks or building blocks surfaced with plaster and separated from the outer leaf of bricks or stone blocks by a cavity about 2in (50mm) wide.

When tapped, a cavity wall sounds solid. For fastenings, treat it as a solid wall (see **page 120**).

Finding verticals Use a plumb line to mark a vertical line on a wall. Tap a nail into the wall where you want the vertical to be, and tie the plumb line to it. When the line is steady, hold a scrap of wood on the wall so it just touches the string and mark the wall at this point. Repeat the procedure at a couple of other places. Alternatively, rub the plumb line with chalk. When it stops swinging, press it against the wall, then pluck the string to leave a vertical chalk line on the wall.

④ Drilling Holes for Screws
Above: **Drill a clearance hole and countersink it.** *Below:* **Pilot hole is slightly less than screw length.**

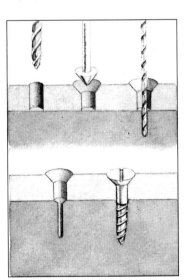

⑤ Skew Nailing for Strength
Assemble frames by skew nailing (driving nails at an angle). The joint will not then pull apart.

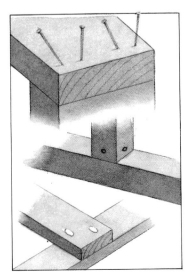

⑥ Using a Nailset
For a neat finish, use a nailset to drive nail heads below the surface, then fill indentation.

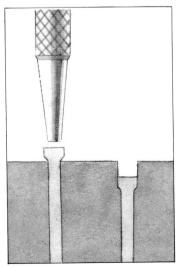

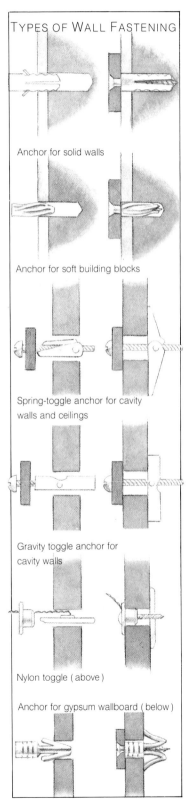

TYPES OF WALL FASTENING

Anchor for solid walls

Anchor for soft building blocks

Spring-toggle anchor for cavity walls and ceilings

Gravity toggle anchor for cavity walls

Nylon toggle (above)

Anchor for gypsum wallboard (below)

Hinges and Catches

Flush hinges These are simply screwed to the edge of the door and the frame, and require no recessing. However, they cannot be adjusted after fitting. Screw the inner hinge flap to the edge of the door, and the outer flap to the inner face of the frame (fig. 1).

Fit the hinges at equal distances from the top and bottom of the door. With a tall or very heavy door, fit a third hinge centrally between the other two. Mark the hinge positions on the edge of the door with the hinge knuckle (joint) in line with the door front. Drill pilot holes and screw on the inner flap. Hold the door in place or rest it on something to raise it to the correct height, making sure that it is accurately aligned top and bottom, and mark the positions of the hinges on the frame. Remove the door and extend these lines using a try square. Hold the door against the frame in an open position, and screw the outer hinge flaps to match up to the guide lines.

Butt hinges These are conventional flapped hinges and are available in steel or in brass (better for high-quality work). They are fitted in the same way as flush hinges, except that the hinge flaps have to be recessed using a chisel or router.

Mark out the hinge positions as for flush hinges, making sure that the hinges are not positioned so that the screws will go into the end grain of cross members.

Mark the length of the hinge using a mat knife. Then mark the width of the hinge and the thickness of the flap using a marking gauge. With a chisel held vertical and a mallet, cut down around the waste side of the recess, then make vertical cuts across the full width of the recess. Chisel out the waste, then pare the bottom of the recess flat using the chisel held with its flat side down (fig. 2).

If you are careful, you can remove the bulk of the waste using a straight bit in a router is set to the depth of the recess. The corners can then be finished using a chisel.

Catches With conventional flush or butt hinges, magnetic catches are popular. The magnet is fitted to the side of the cabinet and the catch plate is then positioned on the magnet. The door is closed on to the catch and pressed hard so that the catch plate marks the door. The door is opened and the catch plate is then simply screwed to the door.

Magnetic touch latches consist of a striker plate that is screwed to the door and a magnetic latch screwed to the frame. The magnet is attached to the end of a small spring housed in the latch; by pushing on the front of the door, it pulls away from the magnet and opens.

Ball catches are very neat devices. On the central edge of the door a hole is drilled to accept the body of the ball catch. The striker plate is then carefully positioned to coincide with the center of the ball.

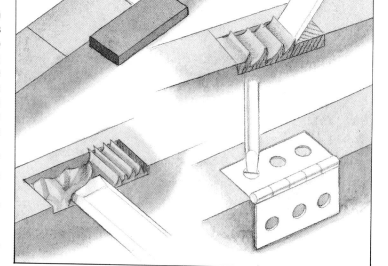

2 The Stages in Fitting a Butt Hinge
Using a try square and a utility knife, mark out the length of hinge. With a marking gauge mark width and thickness of hinge flap. With chisel vertical, cut around outline of hinge. Make series of cuts across width of recess. Pare out waste then check that flap lies flush. Screw the butt hinge in place.

1 Fitting a Flush Hinge
Flush hinges are very easy to fit. Screw the outer flap to the frame and the inner flap to the door.

3 Fitting a Butt Hinge
Butt hinges must be recessed into the door and frame so that hinge flaps are flush with surface.

4 Magnetic Cupboard Catch
A magnetic catch is screwed to the inside face of a cabinet and the catch plate is screwed to the frame.

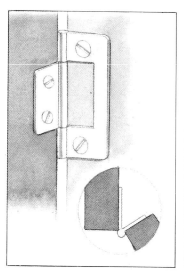

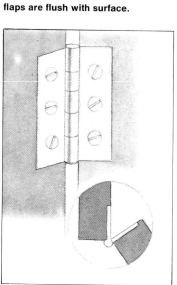

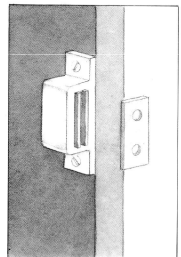

WOOD JOINTS

Butt joint This is the simplest frame joint of all. The ends of the timbers to be joined must be cut square so that they butt together neatly. Corner and T joints can be glued and nailed for strength.

Half-lap joint Also known as a halving joint, these may be used to join wood of similar thickness at corners or to T or X joints (fig. 5). The joint is formed by cutting each piece to half its thickness. Use a try square to mark the width of the cut-outs and a marking gauge set to half the thickness of the wood to mark their depth. Be sure to cross-hatch the waste wood with a pencil so that the correct side is removed. To form a corner half-lap, hold the lumber upright in a vise and saw down to the line, then place the lumber flat and saw across the shoulder to remove the waste. To form a T or X half-lap, saw down each side of the T cut-out to the depth of the central gauge line, and then chisel out the waste wood.

5 Types of Half-lap Joints
Top: **A corner half-lap joint.** *Bottom left:* **A T-half-lap joint.** *Bottom right:* **A cross-lap joint.**

Dado joint Used mainly for shelving, this is simply a slot into which a shelf fits. The "through" dado joint goes to the full width of the shelf, where as a "stopped" dado joint is taken part of the way across the board (fig. 7). Chisel the waste away from each side. In the case of a stopped dado, chisel the waste from the stopped end first. If you have a power router, it is easier to cut a dado joint by running the router across the board against a batten which is clamped tightly at right angles to the board.

Rabbets These are L-shaped steps in the edge of a piece of wood.

By hand Use a marking gauge to mark the rabbet width across the top face of the piece of work and down both sides. Mark the depth of the rabbet accurately across the end and both sides.

Hold the lumber flat and saw down on the waste side of the marked line to the depth of the rabbet. Chisel out the waste one bit at a time along the end grain.

7 Types of Dado Joints
Top: **A through dado joint;** *Middle:* **Through dado joints on the side of a central support;** *Bottom:* **A corner dado joint.**

6 Stages in Forming a Through Dado Joint
Mark width of the dado according to thickness of wood being joined. Use a utility knife. Mark depth with marking gauge. Cut down sides with tenon saw. Chisel out the waste, working from both sides to the middle.

With a router It is not necessary to mark out the rabbet unless you want a guide to work to. However, do practice on scrap wood to be sure of setting the router correctly.

If using a straight cutter, adjust the guide fence on the router so that the correct width is cut, then plunge and adjust the cutting depth so that the router will cut to the correct depth. When the router is correctly set up, simply hold it flat on the piece of work and move it against the direction of the cutter's rotation.

If you are using a cutter with a guide pin, simply adjust the depth of cut and then run the cutter along the edge of the wood to form the rabbet. The cutter will follow irregularities in the wood, so make sure your wood is perfectly straight.

Miter joint This is a type of butt joint, but the faces are cut at an angle (fig. 8). A simple miter joint is glued and nailed, a stronger one is made using dowels, or by sawing oblique cuts into which wood veneers are glued. Cut the joints at 45 degrees using a miter box.

8 Forming Miter Joints
Glue and nail together a simple miter joint. Reinforce with a corner block, dowels, or wood veneer.

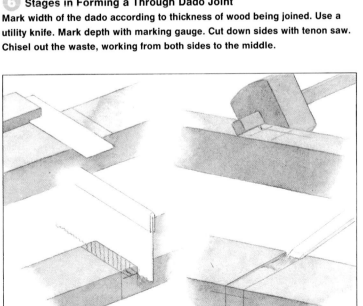

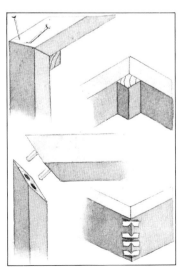

TECHNIQUES: WOOD JOINTS

Dowel joint Dowels are a strong, simple, and hidden means of joining wood together (fig. 1).

Use precut grooved dowels with beveled ends (*see* **Materials, page 117**). These range from ¼in (6mm) diameter by 1in (25mm) long to ⅜in (10mm) by 2in (50mm). The dowel length should be about one-and-a-half times the thickness of the wood being jointed. If you need to use doweling of a larger diameter (as used in the Painting Table project, page 58), cut your own from lengths of dowel. Cut grooves down the length of dowel to allow glue and air to escape, and bevel the ends. When making your own dowels, their length can be twice the thickness of the wood.

On both pieces of wood, use a marking gauge to find the center line, and mark with a pencil. Drill the dowel holes to half the dowel length with the drill held in a drill stand, or aligned with a try square stood on end. Drill the dowel holes in one of the pieces to be joined, insert center points in the holes, then bring the two pieces of the joint together so they are carefully aligned. The center points will make marks in the second piece of wood where the dowel holes should be drilled. Drill the holes to half the length of the dowels, plus a little extra for glue. Where dowels are used for location rather than strength, such as for joining worktops, set the dowels three-quarters into one edge and a quarter into the other.

Put adhesive in the hole and tap dowels into the holes in the first piece with a mallet. Apply adhesive to both parts of the joint; bring the pieces together and clamp them in position until the adhesive has set.

Using a doweling jig A doweling jig enables accurate dowel holes to be drilled. It is clamped over the workpiece above the premarked hole centers. A bush of the same diameter as the drill bit is selected and fitted on the jig. The bush holds the drill vertically as the hole is made. A depth gauge ensures that the hole is the required depth (fig. 4). The jig is then set up on the matching piece of wood and the process repeated.

① Types of Dowel Joint
Dowels can join panels edge to edge and join frames at corners. They can be hidden or have ends exposed.

② Dowels to Join Panels
Right: Mark dowel positions. Drill holes, insert center points. Mark second piece. Dowel together.

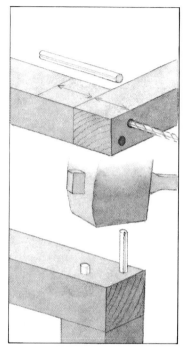

③ Making a Doweled Frame
If edge of frame will not be seen, drill holes for dowels after making frame. Hammer dowels home; cut ends flush after glue dries.

④ Using a Doweling Jig
If dowels are to be hidden, a doweling jig makes it easy to drill holes that align in both pieces.

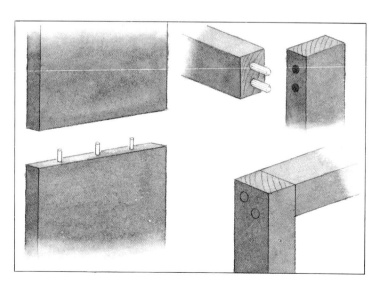

SAFETY

Hundreds of thousands of accidents occur in the home every year. Many of these are the result either of adults undertaking do-it-yourself tasks or of children playing in unsafe environments. Before making any of the projects in this book, always observe the following recommendations.

ADULT SAFETY

Never rush a woodworking or other kind of home improvement job: make sure that you know exactly what skills, tools, and materials you will need *before* you start work. This means reading the project instructions, researching any techniques you are unfamilar with, and, if necessary, practicing first on a piece of scrap wood. Check that you have the right tools, and that they are in good working order. If, for any reason, you are borrowing or renting a tool, read the instructions carefully before you use it, and, again, practice first on a piece of scrap wood.

A clean, tidy work area will enable you to work more quickly and in greater safety: remove waste and clutter at regular intervals. Take special care when using power tools, and always unplug them when they are not in use. Keep children away from your work area, and warn them that your tools and materials are not toys to be played with. The rule of never leaving tools lying around is a fundamental one to observe if there are children in the house. Try to keep your work area well-ventilated, especially when you are using paint, varnish, or solvents.

Wear sensible clothing. Remember that clothes are likely to get torn or dirty. Choose something old, but also consider how you can best protect yourself. Depending on the job, you may need: goggles or safety glasses to protect your eyes; a mask to protect against dust or fumes; gloves to protect your hands when handling, for example, glass; and sturdy footwear for a firm footing. Overalls are often the safest and most comfortable choice of general clothing.

Paint, turps, varnish, and many preservatives are toxic, so treat them with care. Any item being built for use in a child's room or to be played with by a child should be decorated using non-toxic paint and varnish – this is particularly important for the Cradle project (pages 20–25). The lead content in these products is now limited by law (for this reason never use up paint that might have been lying around for years), but paints and varnishes labelled "non-toxic" must not contain any heavy metals at all.

MATERIALS

When choosing your materials, always buy the best you can afford. It is not only much more difficult to make the projects in this book if the faces do not meet properly, it is also more difficult to mark and cut out joints accurately, and more time-consuming, since you will have to plane down all the faces to remove splinters etc.

CHILD SAFETY

Many children sustain serious injuries simply by falling over toys left lying around the house: storage solutions such as the Swing-door Wardrobe (pages 64–73) or the Storage House (pages 32–7) encourage children to be as tidy as possible. Other accidents occur when children play with toys or furniture that have not been made with children in mind. Make sure that a child's toys are age-appropriate, and throw away broken toys. Remember: No room where a child sleeps or plays is safe without a smoke detector.

CONSTRUCTION

Corners and edges should be smoothed and rounded over wherever applicable: the edges of the panels in the Swing-door Wardrobe must be kept flat and square for the door to shut properly, whereas the exposed edges of the Rocking Chair (pages 26–31) can all be rounded over without the design being compromised. Screw heads should always be countersunk, and nail heads punched below the surface to reduce the risk of cuts or injury: use filler to cover the holes and, when it is dry, sand smooth.

Hinged items always present the risk of entrapment, usually of hands and fingers, feet and toes, but sometimes of a child's head; the latter usually occurs when very young children are holding on to a box with a hinged lid and are reaching inside. To minimize the risk, always make the space between the two hinged panels or surfaces either less than $\frac{1}{4}$in (5mm) or greater than $\frac{1}{2}$in (12mm). If you are hinging a lid (a toy box, for example), bear in mind that a child may sustain additional injuries from the force and weight of the falling lid – in extreme circumstances, this has resulted in child fatalities. For this reason, always fit a spring-loaded lid support that will support the lid in any position. Children have also been known to become trapped inside toy boxes, so it is an excellent idea to drill adequate ventilation holes in the sides of any toy boxes.

FURNITURE

Bear in mind that robust, active children climb up and over all manner of surfaces not really intended for such treatment. Even the most vigilant parent or guardian will be unable to provide uninterrupted supervision, so try to anticipate hazards and reduce the risk of injury.

Children will use shelves, tables, chairs, and open drawers in chests of drawers as steps to climb up. In children's rooms, especially, try to keep as much furniture as possible low down, and always use angle brackets or wall anchors to anchor large pieces of furniture to the wall so that there is no chance of them tipping over and causing injury. Bear in mind the weight of the door in the Swing-door Wardrobe project, and make sure that enough magnetic catches are fitted to hold it shut. If you build the Shelf, Rail, and Peg Storage (pages 38–41), think about the age of children using the room before deciding the height at which to screw the boards to the wall.

The Cradle project is designed for a newborn to 3-month-old baby (or whenever an infant can roll over.) If you want to make a larger crib or bed for an older child, you must first investigate safety recommendations concerning spacing of slats, stability, and the risks of strangulation.

TOYS

Toy safety is a serious matter. With common sense, many of the potential hazards such as sharp points or edges can be avoided. Beware of small, detachable parts, which babies and children might choke on, and make sure that rattles are large enough that they cannot become lodged in a baby's throat. Check the lead content of any paints you might want to use to decorate toys: the level of lead is now strictly controlled, but paint sold for use on metal furniture still has a relatively high lead content and should therefore never be used to paint toys.

The projects in this book have all been designed and tested for strength and stability. For this reason you should not modify the designs without first consulting safety guidelines and recommendations for toys and nursery equipment. For up-to-date information, write or call:

U.S. Consumer Product Safety Commission, Washington, DC 20207 (800-638-CPSC or 301-504-0580);

Juvenile Products Manufacturers Association, 2 Greentree Center, Suite 225, PO Box 955, Marlton, NJ 08053 (609-985-2878).

INDEX

ACKNOWLEDGMENTS

The publisher would like to thank the following for their help:

For their ideas, contributions and general assistance:
Hilary Bird; Bridget Bodoano; Joanna Bradshaw; Michelle Clark; Judith Harte; David Jenkens; Madeleine O'Shea; Sean Sutcliffe, Wendy Jones, Kevin Adams, Terry Bartholomew, Jon Cook, Leigh Harrhy, Mark Hinton, Steven Huzzey, and Steve Stonebridge at Benchmark Woodworking Limited; Servis Filmsetting; and Will Webster.

For lending props used in the special photography on pages 18–41 and 50–89:
Alvin Ross/Alfie's Antique Market, 13–25 Church Street, London NW8; The Conran Shop, Michelin House, 81 Fulham Road, London SW3; Decorative Living, 55 New Kings Road, London SW6; Judy Greenwood Antiques, 657 Fulham Road, London SW6; Meaker & Son, 166 Wandsworth Bridge Road, London SW6; Mothercare UK Ltd; The Nursery, 103 Bishop's Road, London SW6; Papers and Paint Ltd, 4 Park Walk, London SW10; The Puffin Children's Bookshop, 1 The Market, Covent Garden, London WC2; Gail Rose; The Singing Tree, 69 New Kings Road, London SW6; The Tintin Shop, 34 Floral Street, London WC2.

For taking part in the special photography:
Rory Higham; Ellie and Sam Johnson; and Lily Whitfield.

Finally, the publisher would like to thank the Royal Society for the Prevention of Accidents for their help and advice about safety in the design and manufacture of toys and children's furniture, and for checking the projects in this book.

PHOTOGRAPHIC ACKNOWLEDGMENTS

The publisher thanks the following photographers and organizations for their kind permission to reproduce the photographs in this book:

9 Peter Aaron/Esto; 11 Marianne Majerus; 12 Yves Duronsoy; 13 below left Yves Duronsoy; 13 right Christian Sarramon; 14 Lewis and Gould Architects, New York (Michelle Lewis); 16 above left Marianne Majerus; 16 below right Yves Duronsoy; 16 below left Yves Duronsoy; 17 Marianne Majerus; 44 left Mark Darley/Esto; 44 center Tom Leighton; 45 Marianne Majerus; 46 right Mark Darley/Esto; 47 right Trevor Richards; 48 Dia Press; 49 left Camera Press; 49 right Jeremy Cockayne; 91 Camera Press; 92 left Gary Rogers; 92 center Dia Press; 92 right Ron Sutherland/Garden Picture Library; 93 Pia Tryde; 94 Georges Lévêque; 95 left Marianne Majerus; 95 right Georges Lévêque; 112 Lars Dalsgaard; 113 Dia Press.

The following photographs were taken specially for Conran Octopus:

Richard Foster 1–7, 18–42, 50–90, 98–111

Shona Wood 8 left (wall units designed and built by Tim Rose), 8 right, 13 above left, 15, 44 right (designed by Georgina Godley), 10 left and right (John, Meryl and Rosie Lakin), 10 center (conceived by Elizabeth Philian and built by Mark Vidler) 16 above right (furniture by Gérard Rigot, design and fittings by Simon Foxell), 43, 47 left (Paxton Locher Architects), 44 right, 46 left (Rebecca Langton).

The publisher thanks the following for their kind permission to reproduce their work on the cover:

Illustrations by Paul Bryant

Photography by:
Richard Foster (above, center left, and below right) and Marianne Majerus (center right and below left).